Vincent McDougall 06/05

The Book of
DANIEL

The Man
The Interpreter
The Prophet

by
John Heading

GW00501509

Walterick Publishers
P.O. Box 2216
Kansas City KS 66110-0216

ISBN 1-884838-14-6

Copyright © 1997 Walterick Publishers

Originally published by Everyday Publications

Cover art by Gary Glover

Maps by Paul Young

List of Contents

THE BOOK OF DANIEL

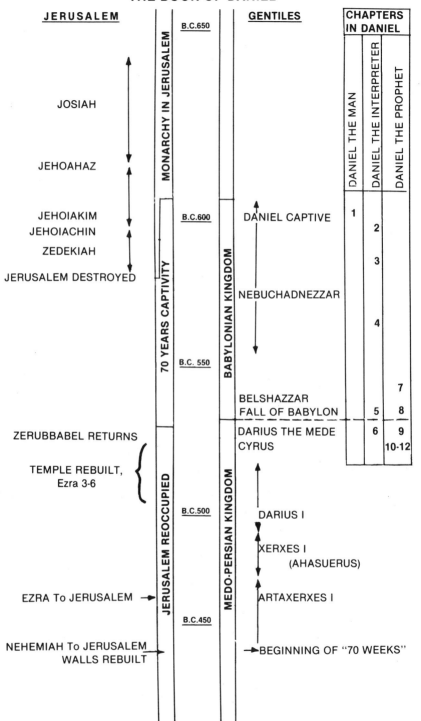

Preface

During 1981, the author was privileged to conduct a weekly Bible Study Meeting in Aberystwyth, Wales, when the Book of Daniel was considered in detail. Prior to discussion on the verses for the week, he gave an introduction, placing the passage in its context. Students could be present only during term time, and holiday visitors only for a week or two, so he found himself repeating his introductory remarks, which tended to range far and wide over the Book of Daniel. Those present wanted to know far more than the details under discussion for the week. In fact, he detected a great lack of knowledge about a Book so fundamental to prophecy and to the understanding of the times of the Gentiles. As with his previous books written under similar circumstances, he decided to write the weekly studies in book form, so as to reach a larger number of Christians who may desire to have a clearer appreciation of the Book of Daniel. This modestly sized book is the outcome. It may be read in conjunction with the author's previous book "From Now to Eternity - the Book of Revelation" available from the same publishers.

The fascination of prophecy is one of the least reasons for studying the subject. The fact that prophecy declares the ultimate glory of Christ in the scene where He was rejected is the primary reason; its moral importance is also a compelling reason for its study. "Watch therefore: for ye know not what hour your Lord doth come," said the Lord in Matthew 24.42. "Hating even the garment spotted by the flesh," wrote Jude in verse 23. "Come out of her, my people, that ye be not partakers of her sins," said a voice from heaven, Rev. 18.4. "What manner of persons ought ye to be in all holy conversation and godliness," wrote Peter, 2 Pet. 4.11. These, and many other verses, show that prophecy should react on the heart, walk and work, as well as on the mind of the believer.

So the author trusts that the Lord will bless the reading of the Book of Daniel by His people. May their understanding of the Book lead to a sanctified yet serving life, glorifying now the One who shall be manifested in glory at the appropriate time in God's future programme.

John Heading

Introduction

Some parts of Scripture give rise to more speculation and imaginative interpretation than do others. For this reason there is a danger of a Christian adhering to the first suggested scheme of prophecy that he comes across, without weighing the whole of the prophetic Scriptures very carefully, a spiritual task that takes a considerable time. The Book of Daniel is largely discredited by rationalists and theologians, who insist that it was written somewhat after the Syrian king Antiochus Epiphanes who passed off the scene of history in B.C. 164, because chapter 11 is so true to historical fact, tracing events between the fall of the Babylonian empire and the evils of Antiochus. They assert, therefore, that the Book consists of stories, legends and myths, written to comfort others who might have to pass through similar tribulation, but that they were never intended to be prophetical.

The study of prophecy has often been descredited by linking prophetical details with events in the present church era. Thus the millennium has been equated to Constantine's edict of toleration; Jerome asserted that the coming of the anti-Christ was near on account of the crumbling of the Roman empire; Augustine stated that the millennium corresponded to the imperial catholic church; the pope has been regarded as Daniel's little horn and the anti-Christ; the catholic church has been heralded as the holy new Jerusalem on earth; Napoleon and the League of Nations have both been branded as the beast of Revelation 13.1-8; Hitler, Russia and the Common Market, and so on, have all been used as they enter the pages of history. The obvious lesson is, "Don't speculate." What we do know is that we are living in the last times, and that the coming of the Lord draws nigh.

Christians should reject all schemes of prophecy (i) if they do not distinguish between the Jew, the Gentiles and the church of God, 1 Cor. 10.32; (ii) if they do not distinguish between God's heavenly purpose for the Church, and His purpose to bless Jews and the nations on earth in a future day; (iii) if they do not foresee God's vindication of Christ in the very scene in which He was rejected.

The existence of prophecy is a miracle from a past era (and that is why it is disregarded by rationalists). It was in the prophets that the Spirit of

God "did signify," 1 Pet. 1.10-12; prophecy came "in old time" not by the will of man, "but holy men of God spake as they were moved by the Holy Spirit," 2 Pet. 1.21; "this we say unto you by the word of the Lord," 1 Thess. 4.15. And yet prophecy can be misunderstood, as with so many other parts of Scripture. Contending for something misunderstood does not make the interpretation correct! In Acts 1.6, the apostles thought that "at this time" the Lord would restore the kingdom of Israel, namely that He would overthrow the Roman domination of their country; the Pharisees thought that the kingdom of God would come with outward show, Luke 17.20; in 1 Corinthians 15 the church denied the resurrection of the body owing to mental difficulties concerning this concept; the believers in Thessalonica had been deceived into thinking that the day of the Lord had already come, 2 Thess. 2.2; some rationalists concluded from the uniformity of nature that the Lord would never come to intervene in the onward course of nature, 2 Pet. 3.4.

God's method in predicting future events must not be overlooked. In many cases, local events in the experience of a prophet are blended with far-future events. In Matthew 24.1-5, the temple in Jerusalem and its forthcoming destruction in A.D. 70 blended with events at the end times. In Revelation 2-3, local errors in the seven churches were so presented as to provide a symbolical account of church history from Acts 2 to the rapture. In Daniel, the 70 years of captivity of the Jewish nation led on to the 70 weeks of prophecy ending with the ultimate restoration, Dan. 9.2,24-27.

The Origins and Dispensations Involved

Eternity looked forward to Christ and the Church: "Christ . . . foreordained before the foundation of the world," 1 Pet. 1.20; "he hath chosen us in him before the foundation of the world," Eph. 1.4. The O.T. looked forward (i) to local events, "these nations shall serve the king of Babylon seventy years," Jer. 25.11; "after seventy years . . . I will visit you . . . in causing you to return to this place," 29.10, (ii) to the Lord's birth, life, death, resurrection and ascension, (iii) to the Gentile kingdoms in the Book of Daniel, (iv) to the future day of the Lord and to Messiah's kingdom. In the N.T., the Lord's teaching embraced every aspect of prophecy, as did the teaching afterwards of the ministers of the Word in local churches, "in the last days perilous times shall come," 2 Tim. 3.1; "as ye have heard that antichrist shall come," 1 John 2.18; "the things which shall be hereafter," Rev. 1.19.

The interpretation of the Book of Daniel goes hand-in-hand with that of the Book of Revelation, for which there exist differing schools of prophecy. There is the *preterist* school, which asserts that the Book of Revelation was fulfilled in the early years of Christianity, and its scheme works mainly without the necessity of the miraculous. Then there is the *historicist* school, that states that the Book of Revelation was fulfilled throughout the Christian era; this requires an extraordinary imagination picking its way through the details of past history. Finally, there is the *futurist* school, asserting that Revelation 4 onwards deals with events in heaven and judgments on earth all in the end times. This third interpretation sees the righteousness of God on earth maintained through judgment. There are also various ideas about the millennium. The *a-millennialist* conceives of Revelation 20 as referring to the church age. The *pre-millennialist* takes Revelation 20 literally, where we have the Lord's second advent in glory taking place just *prior* to the millennium. Finally, the *post-millennialist* sees a golden age to come, but places the Lord's advent *afterwards*. The present writer sees the whole of Scripture consistent with the *futurist pre-millennial* point of view, and the Book of Daniel will be thus expounded.

Readers of prophecy must have very clear ideas about the origin, the present character, and the future of Jews, Gentiles, and the Church of God. Their respective origins are to be found in the call of Abram, Gen. 12.1-2, in the tower of Babel, Gen. 11.9, and in God's eternal purpose finally manifested openly in Acts 2. Their destinies respectively are to be found in millennial blessings and supremity, in subjection to the rule of Christ, and to be associated with Christ as the bride for His eternal satisfaction, Eph. 5.25-27.

O.T. prophecy deals with the Jews and the nations, but not with the Church. It often deals with events up to the time of the Lord Jesus on earth, and then continues in the period of future judgment prior to the establishment of the millennial kingdom. Thereby the church age is passed over in silence, though of course it is to be seen typically in the tabernacle, temple structures and their service. This absence of the church age in O.T. prophecy constitutes a *gap*. Readers of the N.T. can see where this gap must fit into various O.T. prophetic passages. Thus in Daniel 9.24-27 there are 69 weeks (or 483 years) from the decree to rebuild Jerusalem in B.C. 445 to the events surrounding the crucifixion of Christ; after that comes the gap prior to the 70th week (7 years) between the rapture of the Church and the millennial reign.

To understand the Book of Daniel this gap must be appreciated. Thus this gap enters between Daniel 7 verses 7 and 8, where the Roman beast of old is described, followed immediately by the "little horn" of future days. The Lord's life as seen in the O.T. often merges with events after the Church has been taken. Thus in Isaiah 61.1-2 and Luke 4.18-19 we read of His life up to His object "to proclaim the acceptable year of the Lord"; only in the Isaiah passage is the gap evident, for the next phrase refers to the future, "and the day of vengeance of our God." Again, in Isaiah 9.6 we read, "For unto us a child is born, unto us a son is given: (gap) and the government shall be upon his shoulder." The Lord interpreted the gap in Acts 1.6-8; the restoration of the kingdom is still future, but during the intervening period the Gospel would go forth by the power of the Holy Spirit.

Thus we must see that Daniel dealt with events in his own day, and with events up to the first advent of Messiah (events concerning his own nation and the nations around); these merged with future events—the judgment and dissolution of the nations together with the introduction of the kingdom of the Stone and of the Son of man, Dan. 2.44,45; 7.13,14. The Church is not mentioned or even visualized, though there are of course many practical lessons for us today.

Summary of the Book of Daniel

In B.C. 606, the third year of Jehoiakim, Jerusalem was taken by Nebuchadnezzar, and Daniel was taken captive as a youth. This was the beginning of the 70 years captivity, Jer. 25.11.

In B.C. 587, Jerusalem and its temple were destroyed.

In B.C. 538, Cyrus took Babylon. This was the end of the Babylonian kingdom, and the beginning of the Medo-Persian kingdom. Darius the Mede was the first ruler.

In B.C. 536, Cyrus became king, and immediately issued a decree for the rebuilding of the temple in Jerusalem. This ended the 70 years captivity. Daniel lived into the first few years of this reign, Dan. 10.1.

A brief outline of the chapters is as follows:

Daniel the Man

Chapter 1. At the beginning of the Book we have the preparation of a faithful, separated youth, together with that of his three companions. This preparation had to take place before any service for God could commence.

Daniel the Interpreter (in chronological order)

Chapter 2. Daniel revealed and interpreted king Nebuchadnezzar's dream of the metallic image, showing the four kingdoms of the times of the Gentiles, followed by the kingdom of the Stone.

Chapter 3. Daniel's three companions refused to worship the king's huge golden image; they were delivered by divine intervention from the burning fiery furnace.

Chapter 4. Towards the end of his life, Nebuchadnezzar testified of his dream of the tree being cut down, and of Daniel's interpretation. The king was insane for seven years until he recognized the authority of God.

Chapter 5. Belshazzar's idolatrous feast on the last night of the Babylonian kingdom. Daniel interpreted the writing on the wall; the king was slain by the Medo-Persian army, and this new kingdom took control of the Babylonian empire.

Chapter 6. King Darius the Mede was tricked to sign a decree that prayer was only to be made through him. So the faithful and aged Daniel was cast into, and rescued from the den of lions.

Daniel the Prophet (in chronological order)

Chapter 7. Daniel now commenced having visions of his own. As an old man he saw four beasts representing the four kingdoms of the times of the Gentiles, followed by the kingdom of the Son of man.

Chapter 8. Daniel had a second vision of the ram and the he-goat, representing the Medo-Persian and Grecian kingdoms. It leads up to the description of Antiochus Epiphanes as a historical type of enmity against the Jewish people in the last days.

Chapter 9. Towards the end of the 70 years captivity, we have Daniel's repentance and intercession for his nation. He then had the vision of the 70 weeks (490 years) leading up to the far future.

Chapter 10. Chapters 10-12 form a connected vision in the third year of Cyrus, the last recorded vision of Daniel. It was a fearful vision in which Persia was to be destroyed with Greece taking over.

Chapter 11. Daniel was allowed to see the history of the king of the north (Syria) and the king of the south (Egypt), leading up to Antiochus Epiphanes king of Syria, who desecrated the temple in Jerusalem and its worship during the years B.C. 168-165. In verse 36 this leads on to the anti-Christ of the future, with warfare raging over the promised land.

Chapter 12. Israel in the last days will be protected by Michael, and the Book ends with various periods of years to be regarded as signs for the faithful in these future days of persecution.

We must admit that not all expositors see eye-to-eye even on the broad interpretation of certain chapters (particularly chapters 7,8 and 11). We are following the point of view of the majority, except in chapter 8. We shall, however, point out briefly where opinions diverge, though this should not be a hindrance to prophetic study; rather, it should be a stimulus to the reader to be willing to think things through for himself.

Part I

DANIEL THE MAN

Chapter 1
Youthful Faithfulness, Education and Separation

Daniel's Schooldays, 1.1,2

1   Faithfulness towards God, education in the school of God, and separation from worldly influences and from the politics of nations are necessary before a believer is called to serve God. Daniel passed through this spiritual process in chapter 1 before his service commenced in chapter 2.

If we assess Daniel's age as 16 when he was deported from Jerusalem to Babylon, then the date in verse 1, "the third year of the reign of Jehoiakim king of Judah," enables us to state that he was born in the 18th year of the reign of the last good king Josiah. In that reign, Josiah had cleansed the temple for the last time, and had reintroduced the observation of the passover feast. Daniel lived for 13 years under this last good king, yet during that time God's wrath would not be quenched, 2 Kings 22.17, and the city would shortly be destroyed. Daniel would then see the contrast between Jehoiakim's evil activity and the good reign of Josiah; yet perhaps as a member of the royal seed, Dan. 1.3, Daniel remained faithful. He would know of Jeremiah's faithful testimony in the city; this prophet's declaration that Jerusalem would be restored after 70 years, Jer. 29.10, remained as a hope in Daniel's heart until his old age, Dan. 9.2.

So Daniel was deported to Babylon by Nebuchadnezzar in the third year of Jehoiakim's reign. (Jerusalem was not destroyed until 19 years later; see 2 Chron. 36.5,11.) Historians raise certain historical difficulties with verse 1, and rationalists insist that the Book of Daniel was actually written several centuries later, and that the writer had got some of his facts wrong! On the other hand believers, who value the prophetic word as inspired by God, have other explanations of these so-called difficulties, though we shall not examine these here. After all, the Lord spoke of "Daniel the prophet," Matt. 24.15, and this should enable believers to accept the Book of Daniel as it is.

Josiah was not the only one to know of this forthcoming judgment, 2 Chron. 34.23-28. To good king Hezekiah it had been predicted, "all that is in thine house . . . shall be carried into Babylon," 2 Kings 20.17; his sons would become servants in the palace of the king of Babylon. Again, the Lord spoke to Manasseh by His servants the prophets, "I am bringing such evil upon Jerusalem . . . I will . . . deliver them into the hand of their enemies," 2 Kings 21.10-15. Previously, when the city had been attacked by the Egyptians and the Assyrians, there had not been utter destruction; but now the time was ripe for Nebuchadnezzar to come up, 2 Chron. 36.6,7, and later after a further 19 years the city and temple were destroyed, v. 19. The king of Babylon was an instrument of judgment in God's hand, as the Assyrians previously had been described as God's "rod, staff, axe, saw," Isa. 10.5,15. All nations thus used by God bore their own responsibility, and were themselves ultimately destroyed.

2   King Jehoiakim was bound in fetters and carried away to Babylon, 2 Chron. 36.6; this was "surely at the commandment of the Lord," 2 Kings 24.3. He later returned to Jerusalem, and after his reign of 11 years, his son Jehoiachin took the throne for three months, when he too was taken to Babylon. After 37 years, he was released from prison, and formed part of the Lord's regal genealogy, 2 Kings 25.27; Matt. 1.11,12.

The "vessels of the house of God" were carried away into Babylon. They were placed "in his temple," 2 Chron. 36.7, and in "the treasure house of his god." Previously, Shishak king of Egypt had taken away "the treasures of the house of the Lord," 2 Chron. 12.9. Yet the vessels were holy unto God, Exod. 40.9,10, and even the Levitical servants of the sanctuary were not to come near "the vessels of the sanctuary and the altar," Num. 18.3. In other words, the service of the Lord was absolutely holy, and God was a jealous God to maintain this holiness in service. Nevertheless, the king of Babylon placed these most holy things in his idol's temple, as the ark had been placed in Dagon's house previously, 1 Sam. 5.2. These holy vessels were later used in Belshazzar's most idolatrous feast, Dan. 5.3.

Today, this kind of activity is often manifested in the religious world; the things of God are mixed with idolatry. A veneer of Christianity in Christendom does not justify the mixture. The Word of God is taken up in theological circles and treated destructively; the breaking of bread is turned into a resacrifice of Christ; prayer is turned into a repetitive and mechanical occasion; baptism is turned into infant baptism; the Lord Jesus, in the holy vessel of His flesh, was cast out by men, and today they theorize every false insinuation about His Person. Believers must not let the holy things slip from their grasp, thus to become embedded in unholy affections for the world. They should shun all activities in which holy things are imported and used in unsanctified ways. The vessels of gold and silver must remain in holy surroundings, 2 Tim. 2.20, since a believer is "a vessel unto honour, sanctified, and meet for the master's use, and prepared unto every good work," v. 21. Every believer should ensure that he remains a vessel in the house of God, not being ensnared into conditions of darkness without, 2 Cor. 6.14-18.

Daniel's Education and Babylonian Subtlety, 1.3-7

3   In Babylon, Ashpenaz was master of the king's "eunuchs." This word has several meanings in the Scriptures, apart from its normal physical meaning. Such men were court officers, as was Potiphar, Gen. 37.36; 39.1. The same can be said of the man converted on the Gaza road, "a man of Ethiopia, an eunuch of great authority under Candace queen of the Ethiopians," Acts 8.27. Spiritually, some disciples have made themselves "eunuchs for the kingdom of heaven's sake," Matt. 19.12, namely disciples who deliberately keep themselves unspotted from the world.

Amongst these eunuchs in Babylon, there were to be educated some of the children of Israel "of the king's seed," so as to enhance the court of the king of Babylon. Far more than four were selected, as can be seen from verse 6, "among these were . . . Daniel . . . ."

4   The selection of these children was based upon physical appearance plus a good education that had already been profitably received in Jerusalem — the "wisdom, and cunning in knowledge, and understanding science" had been acquired prior to their captivity. This constituted a proof of their ability to learn further, and entry into college today is based on similar considerations.

These new students around the age of 16 were to be taught "the learning and the tongue of the Chaldeans," these men being the ruling caste of priests in the Babylonian temple. Subjects to be taught would include the list: astronomy, philosophy, mathematics, natural history, agriculture, architecture, ancient languages and writing. In addition, there would be included astrology, magic and divination, as well as the special language of the priestly caste. Thus Daniel and his fellows would acquire a good knowledge of the proper science and technology of Babylonian culture of that period, but they would not imbibe the superstitions surrounding these subjects. The ordinary Jew, on the other hand, practising idolatry in Jerusalem, would take in these superstitions without question.

Today, in schools and colleges, young believers may be taught many things contrary to the Scriptures, but they should not accept them as fact! They should take the attitude of Psalm 119.99, "I have more understanding than all my teachers." Moses was learned in all the wisdom of the Egyptians, Acts. 7.22; what was superstitious he would reject, so as to be susceptible to God's teaching throughout the next 80 years of his life. Paul had to face such wisdom in Athens and Corinth, for the Greeks sought after wisdom—but Paul preached "Christ crucified," 1 Cor. 1.22,23, knowing that faith does not stand in the wisdom of men, but in the power of God, 2.5.

5   This class of Jewish young men was to have three years special education in Babylon, after which they would appear before the king for an oral examination, with subsequent selection to be amongst his advisers. The court budget would provide these students with food and drink for these three years, really to make them appear to depend heavily upon the king. As we shall see in verse 8, moral issues were at stake; the food may previously have been offered to Babylonian idols. Daniel would insist upon practical sanctification; he would not depend on the king, and he would take no risks about the purity of the food; "that ye be not partakers of her sins" was his motto, Rev. 18.4. By constant pressure of the environment, the king sought to wean these Jewish scholars from their past lives in Jerusalem (in matters relating to their knowledge and food)—to change their lives so as to absorb completely Babylonian culture and idolatry.

6,7   To achieve further this objective, Ashpenaz changed the names of Daniel and his three friends. This was to seek to obliterate the memory of the spiritual origins of their Jewish names, the new names being designed to attach them closely to Babylonian religion. Today, many unscriptural names are associated with the Christian religion, all distracting from the simplicity that is in Christ. We recall that Joseph's name was changed by Pharaoh to Zaphnath-paaneah, "a revealer of secrets," Gen. 41.45. By marriage, Joseph was brought into the family of the priest or prince of On, such princes retaining land and food allowed by Pharaoh during the famine, 47.22. But Joseph did not imbibe the religion of Egypt, where he lived for the rest of his life.

All the four names that were changed originally contained the name of the true God, and all the four new names contained the names of false Babylonian idols or deities. Thus Daniel (God is judge) was changed to

Belteshazzar (Bel's treasure, or Bel protects the king); see Daniel 4.8, where this new name is stated to be "according to the name of my god." Hananiah (God is gracious, or The gracious gift of God) was changed to Shadrach (Enlightened by the sun-goddess or by the moon-god). Mishael (Who is what God is?) was changed to Meshach (Devotee of Venus, or Who is what the moon-god is?). Azariah (God has helped, or, is keeper) was changed to Abed-nego (Servant of Nego, a Babylonian idol). Their original names are used in 1.19 and 2.17, but their new names are used in 2.49; 3.13,14,16,19,20,22,23,26,28,29,30 in relation to king Nebuchadnezzar.

But their new idolatrous names did not adversely affect their faith; they remained stedfast. They would not "worship the golden image," 3.14; they said, "we will not serve thy gods, nor worship the golden image," v. 18. Believers today should be unaffected by the deviating religious influences that would seek to turn them away from the Lord, for there are always false brethren around who would seek to bring God's people into bondage, Gal. 2.4.

Daniel's Consistency for the Lord, 1.8-16

8 Daniel knew that to partake of the king's food and wine would cause defilement. Or if it *might* cause defilement, then he would not take the risk involved. Perhaps the food had been placed before a Babylonian shrine, or had been offered to an idol, thereby breaking the first commandment, Exod. 20.3. Few believers today seem to realize that partaking of a "toast" at a reception is equivalent to pouring out a drink offering to a god! Perhaps the food was that of an unclean animal, Lev. 11.4-20; perhaps the animal's blood had not been properly removed, Deut. 12.23,24. Hence Daniel would remain loyal to his God and to His revealed law. It appears that all the other Jews except these four did not bother to be consistent with divinely given principles.

Today, believers are surrounded by religious ceremonies and deviations, politics, customs, pleasures, entertainments, and books to gain the mind apart from Christ. Paul describes the enemies of the cross of Christ as those who "mind earthly things," Phil. 3.19, with their affection set "on things on the earth," Col. 3.2. Rather, believers should be satisfied with the Word of God provided by divine inspiration; they should be nourished up in words of faith and of good doctrine, which will lead to being a "good minister of Jesus Christ," 1 Tim. 4.6.

9 The attitude of this prince of the eunuchs to Daniel is remarkable, but only God can move the heart of a heathen man to show kindness to a disciple who is out-and-out for God. For example, in spite of adversity in prison, Joseph's success was because *"the Lord was with Joseph . . . and gave him favour in the sight of the keeper of*

the prison," Gen. 39.21; "*God* was with him . . . and gave him favour and wisdom in the sight of Pharaoh," Acts 7.9,10; "I will give this people favour in the sight of the Egyptians," Exod. 3.21; 11.3; 12.36. Men adopted this attitude towards the Lord Jesus at the start of His life —"Jesus increased . . . in favour with God and man," Luke 2.52. God's will was not always thus; Peter and Paul in The Acts were often regarded as enemies.

10 When Daniel refused the king's food, the prince of the eunuchs thought only of his own life! He was subject to the king, and thought that the appearance of these four men would grow poorer, as if the king's food was bound to make their appearance grow better. This is rationalism at its worst, believing in tradition and natural advantage, rather than putting God to the test by faith, and finding that faith is rewarded.

11 Hence Daniel immediately approached "Melzar" (or "the steward") who was directly in charge of them, a man who was more amenable to mercy, and who would put Daniel's claim to the test. The world can show mercy to God's people on occasions, as when Julius the centurion gave Paul "liberty to go unto his friends to refresh himself," Acts. 27.3.

12 Daniel's request was simple — put the matter to the test just for ten days. They would partake of a diet consisting of pulse (vegetable food) and water only. There was no need for wine, and they refused all meat, not because they were committed vegetarians, but to avoid the dangers of defilement discussed in verse 8. After all, when miraculously feeding the 4,000 and the 5,000, the Lord provided simple, suitable and sufficient food; the appetite and taste of the world need not form the appetite and taste of believers. Hophni and Phinehas loved roast meat, so they manipulated the sin offering (which should be boiled) so that it could be roasted to satisfy their natural palate, thereby rendering unholy the offerings of the Lord, 1 Sam. 2.12-17. The churches at Pergamos and Thyatira were caught up in similar acts of faithlessness, Rev. 2.14,20.

13 Daniel's faith knew what would happen! God was in the matter, and Daniel knew that these four young men could easily be distinguished from their fellows; he willingly testified to the steward that this would be so. It is the same spiritually. When Christians take in the Word and refuse the world, their profiting will appear to all, 1 Tim. 4.15; indeed, it is the Spirit that quickeneth, while the flesh profiteth nothing, John 6.63. The Corinthians were hardly following in Daniel's footsteps; instead of being spiritual, they were acting as "carnal," and Paul found it difficult to distinguish between them and the natural man of the world, 1 Cor. 3.1-3. Today it is easy to discern the difference between one

feeding on the Word and one feeding on the poison of the world, between the consistency of Daniel and the backward behaviour of the rest of the Jews in Nebuchadnezzar's school.

14 The steward took the "risk" for ten days, by listening to the persuasion of a man of God. Not that unbelieving men in authority are always like this! In Acts 27.10, Paul warned of danger to come, but "the centurion believed the master and the owner of the ship, more than those things which were spoken by Paul"; consequently Paul had to say later, "ye should have hearkened unto me," v.21.

15 At the end of the ten days testing, faith and obedience were seen to triumph. The proof of the pudding is in the eating, and this corresponds to the Word of God leading to edification by working effectively in those that believe, 1 Thess. 2.13. The process of spiritual edification by the means that God provides is of tremendous importance; we can prove the matter as Daniel did, following the exhortation of Paul, "Let all things be done unto edifying," 1 Cor. 14.26; 2 Cor. 12.19; 13.10. And not only for ourselves, but what are we placing in the hearts and minds of both saved and unsaved? Do we aim at making a Daniel of others, having proved that we are Daniels ourselves? We need only ten days—a typical period of faithful responsibility that proves that God's ways are right.

16 Even an unsaved man can see a proof when it is obvious! So the steward provided this food regularly for the rest of Daniel's schooling. Of course, in other cases an unsaved man may choose to remain blind even to the most obvious of divine proofs. The Pharisees would not accept the miracles of the Lord, and always wanted proofs by means of further "signs" of a greater and more spectacular nature, Matt. 16.1-4. Neither would Pharaoh accept that the plagues were "the finger of God," Exod. 8.19, in spite of the obvious.

Daniel's Examination, 1.17-21

17 Even if these faithful young men had to imbibe the mythology of the Chaldeans into their minds, it did not enter into the spiritual beings of their hearts. Because they were faithful, God gave them what we may call "superknowledge." God was going to have a man, Daniel, at the commencement of the times of the Gentiles, who would reveal prophetically so much of Gentile history throughout the ages. Mere knowledge according to the flesh could not achieve this, neither could the wisdom of Satan (seen typically in the king of Tyre) who was described as "wiser than Daniel," Ezek. 28.3. Knowledge according to the flesh leads to ignorance of the prophetic future, since men of such ignorance claim that "all things continue as they were from the beginning of creation," 2 Pet. 3.4. And the same difference between spiritual and natural

knowledge applies today. It is the Spirit who gives "the word of wisdom" and "the word of knowledge," 1 Cor. 12.8. Paul claims quite dogmatically that our "faith should not stand in the wisdom of men," 2.5, and that his teaching was "not the wisdom of this world," v.6.

Additionally, Daniel had understanding in "all visions and dreams," the former occurring more particularly (but not always) as sight in waking hours, and the latter occurring in sleeping hours. The Chaldeans had their methods for interpreting dreams, but Daniel was divinely equipped, God having prepared His servant for the tasks ahead. Very few men in the O.T. were thus equipped — Joseph both had dreams and could interpret dreams, Gen. 37.5-11; 40.12,13,18,19; 41.25-36. Men such as Joseph and Daniel were chosen by God at very special times; they formed God's means of speaking to the Gentiles through His servants. In other contexts, God spoke to Solomon in a dream, 1 Kings 3.5; 9.2, and in the N.T. to Joseph the husband of Mary, Matt. 2,13,20,22.

18   At the end of the course, there was the final examination before the king. There were no failures here, since so much devotion to God had been displayed. These four young men had to give an account of themselves to Nebuchadnezzar, and we too must give account to God, Rom. 14.12.

19   The other Jews appeared before the king also, but none of these came out so well in this oral examination. Daniel and his three friends excelled, and all four obtained what we may call first class honours. Our profiting in the school of God must appear before all, and this includes before the secular authorities if necessary. No doubt the king did not understand the origin of this superwisdom; he would learn that in his subsequent experience in the following chapters.

20   This verse describes the actual oral examination. No doubt the "wisdom and understanding" refer to their knowledge of valid Babylonian science, technology and expertise; the king could hardly enquire about the spiritual knowledge of these young men gained from God. Of course, the knowledge of the astrologers was all mixed up with magic, false religion and mythology. Daniel would know all this, but he would never use it in his own teaching. Today we know a lot about worldly things and theories of the rational mind, but we do not use this in our teaching of Scripture, though it is tragic to realize that some believers talk about the creation story in Genesis 1 as a myth. We hear about Bible criticism, evolution, "profane and vain babblings, and oppositions of science falsely so called," 1 Tim. 6.20, but this knowledge must cause us to remain more stedfast in our appreciation of Scripture.

The schooling of Daniel was as necessary for him then as it is for us today, prior to a life of service that is much occupied with prophecy. By faithfulness, we purchase "a good degree," 1 Tim. 3.13, like Ananias, the elders and Demetrius who all obtained a "good report," Acts 22.12; Heb. 11.2; 3 John 12.

21 Such a good beginning in the days of youth accompanies a man of faith throughout life to old age. The believer must maintain the good degree by means of a life consistent with it. In B.C. 606, Daniel was taken captive; in B.C. 587, Jerusalem was destroyed; in B.C. 538, Cyrus took Babylon, while B.C. 536 formed the end of the 70 years captivity. Daniel lived to see the advent of the second world empire, the Medo-Persian empire under Cyrus (chapters 6, 9-12 refer to this second empire, when Daniel was nearly 90 years old). Compare this with many others who started well when God called them, and who afterwards lived and served God for many years, such as Abraham, Joseph, Moses, Joshua, David, Isaiah.

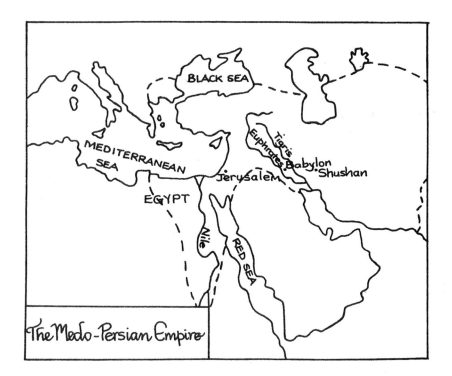

The Medo-Persian Empire

Part II

DANIEL THE INTERPRETER

Chapter 2
Nebuchadnezzar's Dream
and Gentile Dominion

Straightway after his degree, Daniel gained immediate employment. The order is significant, for his first employment was in *the service of God*. His second employment was in *the service of man*, when he was made "ruler over the whole province of Babylon," 2:48. In the lives of young believers today, priorities in the matter of employment should not be forgotten.

Nebuchadnezzar's Dream and the Chaldeans' Impotence, 2.1-13

1 Daniel's education had lasted three years in Nebuchadnezzar's reign, 1.5, yet here at the beginning of chapter 2 we find "the second year" mentioned. Rationalists suggest that the Book was written over four hundred years later, after the rebellious terror perpetuated by Antiochus Epiphanes, and that this later writer got his facts mixed up! Believers in divine inspiration know better, and the figures can be explained by realizing that the Jewish and Babylonian methods for reckoning the years of a reign were different.

The ancients regarded dreams as possessing meanings—not of course following the methods of psychoanalysts today, but by using the methods of interpretation developed by their own astrologers. In the

Scriptures God spoke to some individuals by dreams, as Elihu said, "God speaketh once, yea twice . . . In a dream, in a vision of the night, when deep sleep falleth upon men . . . then he openeth the ears of men, and sealeth their instruction," Job. 33.14-16. Speaking to Moses, Aaron and Miriam, the Lord said that to a prophet "I . . . will make myself known unto him in a vision, and will speak unto him in a dream," Num. 12.6.

Thus at the beginning of the times of the Gentiles, God revealed the forthcoming history of Gentile world-dominion by means of a dream to Nebuchadnezzar. It was so extraordinary that the king had no more sleep that night.

2   The king had at his command this group of magicians, astrologers, sorcerers and Chaldeans, the astrologers using the stars, the sorcerers horoscopes, and the Chaldeans the methods of Babylonian religion. The present writer agrees with those expositors who suggest that the king *had not forgotten* the dream, but that he did not propose to make it known to his advisers. If they through their magic and astrology could show the dream to the king (and he would know whether their claims were true), then he would be able to trust in their powers, and hence he would be able to trust the interpretation that they would also give. But had he told them the dream beforehand, he would have had no guarantee that their interpretation was correct. This was a subtle move on the part of the king, showing that he did not fully trust his advisers. It was not a case of Job 20.8, "He shall fly away as a dream, and shall not be found."

3   The king commenced carefully, merely by stating that he had dreamed a dream that caused him trouble. He let the conversation develop before informing his advisers that it was their responsibility to reveal both the dream and its interpretation.

4   The answer given by the Chaldeans is the beginning of the peculiar structure of the language used in Daniel. Whereas Hebrew is the language of the O.T., yet from verse 4 to the end of chapter 7 the language used is Aramaic. Linguists and theologians may argue without any final agreement as to the reason for this phenomenon, but only when the message of the Book is understood does the matter become clearer. For the subject of these Aramaic chapters concerns more particularly the Gentile nations, and *their* language is used for this purpose. But chapters 8-12 deal with the Jews and with the relationship of the Gentiles with them, and *their* language, Hebrew, is therefore the more appropriate.

The Chaldeans knew their incompetence and limitations. They could not divine the dream, neither could they invent a dream to satisfy the king. What they could do, if they knew the dream, was to use traditional methods of interpretation, and these could have produced a reasonable explanation (though not correct!), whatever the dream's subject matter.

5 The attitude of this merciless dictator was that of absolute barbarity. No doubt he realized that he was giving his advisers an impossible task, but the Babylonian state was not a democracy, and all power resided in the king's hands. He would know whether their disclosure of the dream was correct, else rapid judgment would fall. Their houses were made of earth blocks dried in the sun, and when demolished in heaps, any rain would cause the destroyed homes to become a muddy area, bringing disgrace on the owners. This would be even worse than the fall of a house built on the sand, destroyed by rain and floods, Matt. 7.26,27. If we do not build our doctrine, life and testimony on the rock, then our work can collapse in several ways.

6 Conversely, Nebuchadnezzar would distribute lavish rewards if his advisers fulfilled their obligations. It was so in Joseph's case; Pharaoh said to him, "Thou shalt be over my house . . . Pharaoh took off his ring from his hand, and put it upon Joseph's hand, and . . . fine linen, and . . . a gold chain," Gen. 41.40-42. Similarly, Haman's answer was, "whom the king delighteth to honour," Esther 6.8. For service well done today, believers do not seek any reward from man; Paul and Barnabas rightly refused oxen, garlands and sacrifice, Acts 14.13. The "Well done" comes only from the Lord, and none shall lose his reward in that day.

7 This is the same Chaldean response as in verse 4, except now they realized the impossible situation in which they had been placed by the dictator.

8 Thus the king accused them of playing for time by their answers, putting the matter off by delay, and even trusting that the king would forget his impossible demands. The lesson for believers is obvious; the way in which we conduct our service before men must be such as not to attract any accusations from the world on any justifiable basis. False accusations there may be, as in the case of the Lord's service when the religious leaders always criticized His activity—of course, without any grounds whatsoever except their own bias and prejudice. If we are buffeted for our own faults, there can be no glory, but when we are buffeted for doing well and take it patiently, this is acceptable with God, 1 Pet. 2.20.

9 There are further accusations from the king. The advisers sought delay until "the time be changed," namely until fresh circumstances caused the king to cease to worry about his dream, when his insistence would cease. In the meantime, he stated that these men would prepare "lying and corrupt words." For us, there must be no delay, and there must be wholesome words: we must "be ready *always* to give an answer to every man that asketh you a reason of the hope that is in you,"

manifesting a good conversation before those who accuse us falsely, and suffering for well doing, 1 Pet. 3.15-17.

10 The Chaldeans recognized the impossibility of the king's demands, and they did not hesitate to tell the king so. They confessed the limitations of all men, and that the miraculous was beyond them. For us, we must learn to recognize the limitations of our knowledge or of any particular spiritual gift granted by the Holy Spirit; what has been granted is sufficient for that believer's service.

11 The Chaldeans further confessed that only "the gods, whose dwelling is not with flesh" could reveal the dream. Since their gods were mere images of various materials, the credulity of the heathen is extraordinary to contemplate. In Daniel 3.1, the king's god was a golden image, while in 5.4 the **six** materials "gold, silver, brass, iron, wood, stones" are mentioned. They had no grounds based on past experience for thinking that such gods could reveal dreams. For believers, this description is in contrast to the Lord Jesus. We read of the **seven**-fold Spirit upon Him, Isa. 11.2, and certainly He did become flesh so as to dwell amongst men, John 1.14; 1 Tim. 3.16.

12 The king's anger then showed how much trust he had in his gods! It is easy for a heathen king to worship these gods, but really impossible through experience to trust them for help. The prophets of Baal could not induce him to bring down fire to consume the bullock on the altar, 1 Kings 18.26-29, but how different was the result when Elijah called on the name of the Lord.

13 Consequently, the king resolved to destroy all the men who should have been in contact with their gods. This decree shows the strength and power behind a one-man dictatorship. Those who would carry out this plan interpreted it as including Daniel and his friends. If such were the will of God, they would have been willing to be slain; cf. Dan. 3.17,18. Paul adopted such an attitude when he said, "I am ready . . . to die at Jerusalem," while the disciples said, "The will of the Lord be done," Acts 21.13,14.

Revelation of the Dream to Daniel, 2.14-23

14-16 These verses form Daniel's *public* reaction, while the following verses show his *private* reaction. His "counsel and wisdom" stand in contrast to the king's fury and anger, v.12, and to his haste, v.15. Daniel's character and ability were so well known, that Arioch explained the matter to him. Moreover, Daniel had access to the king, because of his God-given ability; this the king had previously recognized when he had communed with him. Daniel asked for time, v.16, and this was granted, unlike verse 8 where no time was granted to the king's advisers. In other words, an absolute dictator can be inconsistent, and he can have his favourites. Such a king does not need to answer to any man for his inconsistencies and his attitudes. In all that Daniel did, he gave "no offense in any thing, that the ministry be not blamed," 2 Cor. 6.3.

At the end of verse 16, Daniel had confidence that he could supply the king's requirements; this demanded absolute faith in God, a faith that knew that God had given him "understanding in all visions and dreams," 1.17. This was, of course, far above all the learning of the wise men in Babylon. Similarly, our learning of the Scriptures is far more advanced and elevated than all the philosophies and theories of men. We have an unction (anointing) from the Holy One, and therefore know "all things," 1 John 2.20, particularly as He teaches us "of all things," v.27. We must trust in God that His promise will be accomplished in us. When we have a gift from God, we must expect to exercise it by His grace. This is not boasting, but testifying to what He can do in and through His servants.

17 So Daniel returned home, and made the matter known to his three companions; there was fellowship with others who demonstrated similar faithfulness. Thus in Acts 13.1,2, when their work was finished in Antioch, Paul and Barnabas shared in prayer with other teachers and prophets regarding their next work. In Acts 16.9,10 Paul confided in Luke and Silas regarding the vision that they should go to Macedonia. Even the blessed Lord, in Gethsemane's garden, sought the fellowship of the three apostles, that they should tarry and watch with Him, Matt. 26.38.

18 Understanding of the dream would not come by sitting back and taking the ease of the world. There was to be communion in prayer,

(i) for divine mercies,
(ii) that the secret would enable the king to know and to extol the God of heaven, and
(iii) for the safety of these four faithful men.

This was not a selfish wish, but because in their youth they could sense that there was much more for them to do in the Lord's testimony and service in Babylon.

Unity in this prayer was essential; two or three agreeing would ensure an answer to the prayer, Matt. 6.6; 18.19. Thus there was united church prayer in Acts 2.42; there were many gathered together in a home to pray for Peter, 12.5,12; Paul kneeled down and prayed with them all, 20.36.

19 Thus the secret of the dream was revealed to one man, Daniel, not to the other three. There should be no jealousy when God takes up one man, even though others may be just as well qualified and faithful. Daniel used the title "God of heaven," and not the "God of Abraham, Isaac and Jacob." This is because the nation was "Lo-ammi," Hos. 1.9, namely "not my people" since they were idolatrous and apostate. In Daniel's day, there were only faithful individuals.

20 Up to verse 23, Daniel engaged in thanksgiving and prayer **before** going to the king. This is like the one leper, who returned to give thanks to the Lord (namely, to God, this being a proof of His deity) before going to the priest, Luke 17.18. Daniel knew that his knowledge represented the right dream; he did not need Nebuchadnezzar's confirmation of this. The prayer reflects in its subject matter what had been revealed. Thus Daniel said "for ever and ever," based on the truth of the kingdom "which shall never be destroyed . . . it shall stand for ever," Dan. 2.44. The "wisdom" of God manifests His character that had plans to enhance His glory. The "might" refers to the means whereby God would introduce His kingdom, namely, the image would be destroyed.

21 God changes "the times and the seasons." No doubt the "times" imply years, for often a "time" denotes a year, as "a time and times and the dividing of time" denote three and a half years, Dan. 7.25; 9.27; Rev. 12.14; 13.5. Compare Daniel 4.25 where "seven times" means seven years. In other words, God changes circumstances over the years, as kingdom gives place to kingdom throughout the dream-image. Moreover, God "removeth kings, and setteth up kings," this idea being the basic substance of the interpretation of the image. Thus Pharaoh had been raised up by God so that the divine power could be displayed in him, Rom. 9.17, and "no power" exists apart from what is of God, 13.1. Additionally, Daniel confessed that God gives "wisdom to the wise, and knowledge to them that know understanding." In other words, God does not feed deliberate ignorance; "Give instruction to a wise man, and he will be yet wiser," Prov. 9.9. It is a case of John 7.17, "If any man shall do his will, he shall know of the doctrine." Many times the Lord enunciated this truth, "whosoever hath, to him shall be given," Matt. 13.12; 25.29; Luke 19.26.

No doubt this is the reason today why some Christians never seem to make progress—they don't want to. Others do make progress, because there is a spiritual will. Daniel knew of his experience in chapter 1, when such spiritual progress had been made. Here in chapter 2 he was able to receive more. But how necessary had been the preparation in chapter 1.

22 The revealed "deep and secret things" are rooted in the counsels and prophetic knowledge of deity. These things cannot enter into the unsaved heart of man; rather, they are revealed by the Spirit who searches "the deep things of God," 1 Cor. 2.9,10. Thus in understanding the Book of Daniel, for example, the simplest believer has a complete advantage spiritually over every academic theologian who pronounces upon the Book in a critical and destructive way.

Whether open or in secret, whether in darkness or in light, all is known to God, Psa. 139.11,12. No doubt by "darkness" Daniel implied the future religious and political darkness of the nations; God would show it all up beforehand. Once in vision form, Ezekiel had to dig down into a wall, so as to see things done "in the dark," Ezek. 8.7-12. God knew, and guided Ezekiel to see also! Even the light can hide idolatry on occasions, as in verse 16 where Ezekiel saw the worship of the sun taking place in its light, with men's backs turned towards the temple.

23 Daniel had *worshipped* God in verses 20-22, and now in verse 23 he *thanks* God; the order is significant. No longer did the prophet use the title "God of heaven" as when speaking to his friends, v.18, but he used the title "God of my fathers." He valued this divine relationship from the past with faithful men of his nation, regardless of the present state of that nation. The granting of "wisdom and might" took place in chapter 1, and derived from similar, but higher, divine characteristics, 2.20. Again, "(thou) hast made known" refers to what had just taken place in chapter 2. Note the change in pronoun: the revelation of the dream was "unto *me* . . . what *we* desired." *One* had the revelation, but it was intended for *all*, and is very similar to Acts 16.10 where *only Paul* had the vision but then *all* the company endeavoured to go into Macedonia.

Daniel's Testimony to the King, 2.24-30

24-26 Daniel did not have direct access to the king's presence; entry had to be by Arioch. His declaration before the king that he had found a man able to interpret the dream sounds rather strange; only the previous day Daniel himself had been in the king's presence claiming to be able to interpret the dream, v. 16. The king's question to Daniel arose either (i) from Arioch's assertion that he had found such a man, or (ii) from Daniel's own claim the previous day. The king demanded (i) the dream, and (ii) the interpretation. If (i) were correctly described by Daniel (and the king would know whether it was correct from his own knowledge), then (ii) would be correct and trustworthy as based on a miraculous work.

27,28 Daniel testified of his God first, before explaining the dream. His God stood in complete contrast with even the cleverest of men, since no ordinary man could reveal a dream, vs. 10,27. Rather, the revelation would come from "a God in *heaven*," far removed from the military, political and religious exploits of the nations on earth, their leaders, and their wise men. The prophetic character of the dream was stated immediately by means of the words "in the latter days," namely the dream extended up to the time of the end of Gentile dominion over the world's affairs. Paul, too, often took the minds of his readers up to the last times, 1 Tim. 4.1; 2 Tim. 3.1.

29 Daniel moved slowly to the point; he first dealt with the psychology of the king on the night of the dream. On his bed, the king had been thinking about what would happen to his mighty kingdom after his own reign was concluded. This is a thought that has troubled many dictators of the past, and Hitler's own worry about the problem of succession during the last world war comes to mind. God used that very night (namely, very near to the beginning of the Gentile rule) to reveal in dream form what would happen up to the far distant future. It is still revealed in the Word of God to all those whose spiritual ears are opened. Even this piece of "private thought-reading" would convince Nebuchadnezzar that Daniel knew both the dream and its interpretation.

30 Yet in spite of this superior capability, Daniel took a lowly position. The revelation had not been given to enhance his own knowledge, wisdom, status and prestige. He had received the secret so that the interpretation could be made known to the king—and to all readers of the Word of God. "The thoughts of thine heart" can hardly refer to the dream itself, but to his thoughts as he lay awake before he slept.

The Dream and its Interpretation, 2.31-45

31 The pictorial contents of the dream are given in verses 31-35, while its interpretation is found in great detail in verses 36-45. Huge metallic colossi were built in Egypt and Babylon; construction would start from the top, with poorer materials being used lower down. Thus such an image would not be unknown to the king, and might have been quite familiar. What caused the king so much terror was its fearful, sudden, unexpected and unexplained destruction. The description of the image is one of "pre-eminence," an image that seeks to mimic the glory of the Lord Jesus. God allowed the glories of the nations to be seen through Satan's and men's eyes. Later, Satan showed to the Lord Jesus "all the kingdoms of the world, and the *glory* of them," Matt. 4.8, namely what the image was supposed to represent to men's eyes. Therein man could see his own supreme political height, leaders could view their own supremacy that so displaced the glory of the God of heaven.

32,33 The materials, "gold, silver, brass, iron" copied the metallic materials used in the tabernacle and temple, 1 Chron. 29.2. A copy of the best of the metals will form part of the dress and trade of Mystery Babylon of a future era, Rev. 17.4; 18.12. The image forms a horrible copy of the poetic description of the Lord in Song of Songs

5.11-16, which contains a glorious contrast. "His head is as the most fine gold" is followed by hands "as gold rings" and feet of "fine gold" — no diminishing in value here from head to feet! (The image also tends to copy what is valuable in the believer's service, the gold and silver being what is proper to build on the "one foundation . . . , which is Jesus Christ," 1 Cor. 3.11,12) In Revelation 1.15, the Lord's feet are "like unto fine brass, as if they burned in a furnace," while His girdle is a "golden" one. The brass here represents no downward graduation in value, of course, but is a picture of the purity of His walk in judgment as prepared to burn up the dross found in the seven churches. Again, by contrast, in the dream-image God described the end-time kingdoms by "part of iron and part of clay," strength, weakness and no cohesion all being intermingled. Men may glory even in that, but to God such a world-empire is ripe for devouring judgment.

34 Thus the dream ends with a "stone . . . cut out without hands." This stone was entirely separate from the image—it had no human intervention as to its formation or origin (namely, as the king perceived it, for believers know that the Son of God had no formation or origin), and the stone's activity was accomplished without human intervention.

The lower part was broken, so the whole would crumble; a giant political system is as unstable as its foundation. The Lord used the idea of destruction many times in His teaching, although when men talk glibly about His example of love, this opposite side of His teaching is conveniently forgotten. The house built on the sand would collapse, Matt. 7.27; every stone in the temple in Jerusalem would be thrown down, 24.2; while John the Baptist spoke of trees being hewn down, 3.10; see 7.19; Dan. 4.14.

35 All the materials of the dream-image were "broken to pieces together." The following interpretation shows clearly that each kingdom was successively overtaken, so "together" cannot mean "at the same time" but "in the same manner." However, the social structure, culture, and political power of all the kingdoms will be embraced by the one kingdom at the end, so all will then be destroyed. This is the same feature as seen in the four beasts of chapter 7, showing the development of Gentile political power as assessed through God's eyes. One by one these kingdoms passed away, yet "their lives were prolonged," 7.12, implying the successive absorption of the previous kingdoms into the fourth one. This is also seen in Revelation 13.2, where the "lion, bear, leopard" characteristics are all included in the final beast.

Everything is dissipated and carried away; nothing is left to mar the millennial kingdom of the Lord Jesus. The picture of "chaff" is used to describe this carrying-away process, a picture so often used in the Scriptures. The ungodly are like the chaff, Psa. 1.4; so are the wicked, Job 21.7,18; those that opposed David, Psa. 35.5, and even the inhabitants of Jerusalem, Isa. 29.5. The chaff is what Satan wants, Luke 22.31, but the wheat will be found in the Lord's garner, Matt. 3.12.

Thus with the mass of chaff dissipated, there will be no hindrance to the stone filling the whole earth, namely, every place that had been controlled by the kingdoms represented by the metals and the beasts. In that day, "the earth shall be filled with the knowledge of the glory of the Lord, as the waters cover the sea," Hab. 2.14.

36 Daniel then provided the king with the interpretation, vs. 36.45.
Daniel used the form "we" and not "I", as if to remind the king of the faithful group of four young men. It is the "we" of fellowship in divine service, something that characterizes many of Paul's Epistles. May we ask the reader, Did the Lord in His teaching ever use the form "we" so as to embrace His disciples with His service?

37 Daniel dwelt upon the position and power of Nebuchadnezzar before showing him his position in the image. As "a king of kings" he was the first Gentile ruler after the Jews had been placed on one side. There had been empires previously, such as Egypt and Assyria, but then the Jews were still God's people. Nebuchadnezzar's character of cruelty, oppression and expansionism was the opposite to the character of the Lord Jesus as "King of kings." Once again, God's title as "the God of heaven" is used, since He was no longer God of His people as dwelling amongst them upon His throne in Jerusalem. He had given them their nationhood, land, people, glory and blessings until they failed. After that the government of the world would be in Gentile hands, and they failed from the beginning. The later development of Gentile power under Rome would form the background against which the Church would be formed in The Acts, with the divine objective that it should expand amongst the Gentile nations, Acts 1.8. It was only after many years that Nebuchadnezzar's pride was abased so that he could recognize that his position came from God, Dan. 4.25. Strictly all possessions and positions come from God in keeping with His will; we have nothing that we did not receive, 1 Cor. 4.7. In the future, this kingdom, power, and strength, and glory" will be that of the Lord Jesus, when all things will be under His feet, Heb. 2.8, and then will be fulfilled Matthew 6.13, "Thine is the kingdom, and the power, and the glory, for ever."

38 Babylon had previously been described as "the golden city," Isa. 14.4, or, according to the margin, "the exactress of gold," and Nebuchadnezzar is described as "Thou art this head of gold." According to our verse, the king could have been "ruler over them all," though in practice he limited himself to certain conquests and dominions. Solomon had reigned "over all the kings from the river (Euphrates) even unto the land of the Philistines, and to the border of Egypt," 2 Chron. 9.26. But the Lord's kingdom will be limitless.

The Babylonian empire lasted for 66 years; it was characterized by despotic government, the king having absolute control. (Such power-hungry dictators have been scattered through the pages of history.) All nations trembled before him; he slew those whom he would; others he set up and set down, Dan. 4.19. He set up an image all of gold, identifying deity and worship with himself, 3.1, and ultimately became insane in the fields like an animal for seven years, 4.33, until he knew that "the most high God ruled in the kingdom of men, and that he appointeth over it whomsoever he will," 5.21. He was "converted" to praise "the King of heaven," 4.37.

Moreover, Babylon was the lion kingdom of Daniel's dream in his old age, 7.4. It was the first of the four great beasts "diverse one from another," v.3, having "eagle's wings." We shall explain this symbolism in detail when we consider chapter 7, but we may remark here that the nation that destroyed Edom was like a lion and an eagle, Jer. 49.19,22, speaking of the ability to expand and to invade. Nebuchadnezzar's position and status had been given by God, so he had more responsibility towards God, and would suffer more severe punishment. The wings of the first beast were plucked, and a man's heart given to it, 7.4, meaning the king's humiliation, and his conversion from the worship of his image of gold to the true God of heaven. The Babylonian kingdom ended in Daniel 5.30, when "Darius the Median took the kingdom."

39   The image's breast and arms were of silver, speaking of another kingdom "inferior to thee." In other words, a process of devolution immediately set in, such a process being a general law of nature in human society. Evolution to the best is an aspiration of the non-Christian; it is a theory of the rationalist, and strictly entirely non-valid to the Christian. The nations exhibit the same depravity as the human heart; better times and institutions give rise to man's insidious activity to overthrow them—and this applies to today as well as to past history. Thus Belshazzar was found wanting in the gold of the image's neck, and the lower Darius of silver took the kingdom.

The silver empire—the Medo-Persian empire—lasted for just over 200 years. It has been described as bureaucratic government, rule by departments and not by a supreme dictator (as seen when Darius was helpless to save Daniel from the den of lions, 6.14,15. A despot would not have been in the predicament that Darius found himself in!)

This second kingdom is also the "bear" kingdom of Daniel's dream, Dan. 7.5. The bear is stated to be "on one side," or "of one dominion," reflecting upon the unity of Media and Persia. The two parts, breast plus arms, also speak of the unity of the two nations, as do the two horns of the ram in Daniel's second vision, 8.3, stated to be the "kings of Media and Persia," v. 20. It was demanded that the bear "devour much flesh," showing the empire as ferocious, bloodthirsty, massive, cruel and insatiable. The three ribs in its mouth would refer to Libya, Egypt and Babylon. Even while Belshazzar was still alive—before the first kingdom was overthrown—this ram is seen as pushing west, north and south, with none being able to stand before him, v.4. Secular history shows how true this prophetic description really was.

The third kingdom of brass "shall bear rule over all the earth," showing how the world would be subject to God's prophetic program, though the leaders would be entirely responsible for their actions. The history of the third kingdom, that of Greece, does not appear in the historical part of the O.T., since the kingdom existed between the O.T. and the N.T. But the prophetic details are exact when examined in the light of profane history. The military government of Greece was ruled by its first king Alexander the Great; he defeated the Medo-Persian empire in keeping with God's will, using a small army against two and a half million men. This kingdom lasted for about 300 years.

In Daniel's first vision, this is described as the "leopard" kingdom, 7.5, symbolical of art, culture, civilization. Its four wings speak of rapid conquest in all directions; its four heads speak of the four divisions of the kingdom after Alexander's death as a young man. In Daniel's second vision this kingdom is described as a "he goat," 8.5, with a "great horn," v.8. This goat is defined to be "the king of Grecia: and the great horn . . . is the first king," v.21. After him, four other horns arose in four directions, v.8, defined to be the subsequent four kingdoms rising from the original united nation, v.22. This subdivision is also described in 11.4, "his kingdom shall be broken, and shall be divided toward the four winds of heaven." From one of these kingdoms, Antiochus Epiphanes arose, typical of enmity against God's people in the future, 8.9-12; 11.21-32.

40   The fourth kingdom is represented by iron, implying political and military strength to destroy. The Roman emperors were upheld by the Roman army, which broke all in pieces as Rome subdued all the western world. In the first vision of Daniel, this empire was represented *through God's eyes* as the fourth beast, Dan. 7.7. It was dreadful, terrible, strong exceedingly, with iron teeth with which it broke all in pieces, and was diverse from the previous three beasts. No animal of God's creation was suitable to represent pictorially this fourth empire. Rome took over as Greece fell into various pieces prior to the beginning of the N.T. No other world kingdom is predicted in Daniel chapters 2 and 7; this fourth kingdom would terminate the times of the Gentiles, Luke 21.24. After that would follow divine intervention of quite a dif-

ferent kind, when the God of heaven shall "set up a kingdom," with the fourth beast slain and the saints possessing the kingdom, Dan. 7.22.

It was this fourth beast in its relative infancy which crucified the Lord Jesus, that destroyed Jerusalem and the temple, that slaughtered millions of Jews in A.D. 70, that caused the apostle Paul to be martyred, that persecuted the early Christians, and that polluted the church, thereby leading to papal Rome. Prophecy then passes over the church age, "the gap," between the legs and the feet.

41,42   These verses give further details of the image's feet, being part of iron and part of clay, v.33. The ten toes of iron and clay speak of a kingdom partly strong and partly broken. This suggests the character of democracy in the last times; the authorities will not be able to govern unchallenged because of rebellion by some of those governed. No absolutely stable government will exist, as demonstrated by three horns being plucked up, Dan. 7.8, and five kings being fallen, Rev. 17.10.

The final development is seen by the beast having ten horns, Dan. 7.7, an amalgamation of many nations. One little horn, v.8, will take control, with "a mouth speaking great things." At that time, Psalm 2.2 will be fulfilled. "The kings of the earth set themselves . . . against the Lord, and against his anointed." This last great ruler "shall speak great words against the most High," he shall prevail against the saints, wearing them out, Dan. 7.21,25. Finally, the beast shall be slain when the Lord comes in glory, vs. 11,26.

43   In his interpretation, Daniel continued, "they shall mingle themselves with the seed of men" (that is, the toes shall mingle themselves); they "shall not cleave this to that," marg. This suggests that the future leaders shall seek to be democratic (the opposite to Nebuchadnezzar), bringing the people into the decision-making process, but it will not be effective. For at the end there will be the complete degeneration of democracy; the leaders will manipulate the system to reserve all power to themselves, in spite of the outward show and talk of democracy. (Some suggest that the clay refers to the Jews; this metaphor is used in Jeremiah 18.1-6 with this sense, but we feel that these two uses of "clay" are entirely different. In Jeremiah, the clay, [as the Jews] is capable of being formed in God's hands; in Daniel the clay is subject to the iron authorities.)

44   The "days of these kings" refer to the period of the ten toes and the ten horns, 7.24, forming the base of the whole structure. It is only when they meet their end that the kingdom of God is set up in open display. Not until then will this occur, although when the Lord was here the Jews were often thinking that it should happen immediately, the Romans having held sway for only a few decades. The Pharisees thought this, so the Lord said, "The kingdom of God cometh not with outward show," Luke 17.20 marg. The kingdom is moral now, being "within you"; see Luke 2.38; Acts 1.6.

The "God of heaven" speaks of the authority behind His kingdom. Even now, He exercises His divine authority by giving the kingdoms of men to men of His own choice, Dan. 4.17. Thus, in that day, concerning His Christ He will say, "Yet have *I* set *my* king upon my holy hill of Zion," Psa. 2.6.

This final kingdom "shall never be destroyed," and "it shall stand for ever." This is in contrast to the four previous Gentile empires, and is in keeping with Gabriel's promise to Mary, that Jesus would have the throne, that He would reign for ever, and that His kingdom would have no end, Luke 1.32,33. First of all there will be the 1,000 years, Rev. 20.4,5,6, at the end of which the kingdom will be delivered to God eternally, 1 Cor. 15.24.

Moreover, Daniel said, "the kingdom shall not be left to other people." Namely, no longer would a mere human ruler be in control. No ruler like Nebuchadnezzar, Cyrus, Alexander or the Caesars; rather the Ruler will be the Stone, the King of kings and Lord of lords, when "a king shall reign in righteousness," Isa. 32.1.

45 For believers, the stone is a Messianic symbol. But since Daniel did not interpret it, Nebuchadnezzar must have had quite different ideas about it. (i) Since there were no stones in the local Babylonian soil, an outside source would have been suggested — for us, a heavenly source. (ii) In Babylon there was a paved stone way known as the "sacred way," permitting the king to have a religious concept — for us, a spiritual concept of the Lord as the Stone. (iii) Boundary stones were used to mark out corners of land; here the boundary is stated to be limitless — the stone filled the whole earth, v. 35. Moreover, the stone was cut out "without hands," namely the work was entirely divine from heaven. The stone would descend from a mountain, the existing unseen kingdom and purpose of God.

Scripture often uses a stone as a Messianic symbol. For example, "the shepherd, the stone of Israel," Gen. 49.24; "a foundation stone, a tried stone, a precious corner stone, a sure foundation," Isa. 28.16; "the stone . . . on whomsoever it shall fall, it will grind him to powder," Matt. 21.44. Finally, Daniel stated that "the dream is certain"—he knew that he was quoting the right dream, and the king knew also. "And the interpretation thereof sure;" Daniel knew this as coming from God, and he wanted the king to be sure also.

Nebuchadnezzar's Reaction, 2.46-49

46 Some suggest that the king worshipped God through Daniel
        because of verse 47. But verse 46 is clear, "he worshipped
Daniel," and saw fit to offer heathen offerings "unto him," failing to
draw a sharp distinction between Daniel and "your God is a God of
gods." Thus Peter could not be worshipped by Cornelius, Acts 10.26,
and it was quite wrong for John to attempt to worship an angel, Rev.
19.10; 22.9. The men of Lystra sought to do sacrifice to Paul and Barnabas as manifestations of their gods, Acts 14.11-18, but they restrained
the people with difficulty. Paul would keep in a very humble position,
being persecuted and stoned even unto death. But in Daniel's case, it was
God's will for His young servant aged about 19 that he should be
elevated to a position of very high rank in Babylon.

47 The king's great confession was of a God unique in His works,
        but not in His Person. He still acknowledged other gods by say-
ing, "a God *of gods.*" As Paul wrote, "though there be that are called
gods . . . (as there be gods many, and lords many,) but to us there is but
one God, the Father . . . ," 1 Cor. 8.5,6; men may offer sacrifice to idols,
but "we know that an idol is nothing in the world, and that there is none
other God but one," v.4; Exod. 20.3. In Nebuchadnezzar's case, he still
retained his Babylonian gods, though acknowledging the superiority of
Daniel's God, following Daniel's testimony previously of the God in
heaven who reveals secrets, Dan. 2.28.

48,49 Daniel was then granted a two-fold high honour, being placed
        over all the province of Babylon and over the wise men. One can
only accept such high honours when this is according to the will of God.
Daniel did not seek them for himself; he had not sought this as a career,
though he desired that his three friends should be associated with him
closely. It was like the case of Joseph, to whom Pharaoh said, "I have set
thee over all the land of Egypt," Gen. 41.41. No doubt there were temp-
tations in such a high natural calling, but Daniel had already proved that
he could live faithfully and untainted. The relationship between natural
responsibility and spiritual responsibility is discussed by the Lord in Luke
16.10-12.

This is surely a lesson for us today; the believer must avoid dishonest
dealings and activity in his daily occupation, otherwise one's testimony
is dull and not clear-cut. Naaman was not marked by such standards
after his cleansing. He declared that he would not offer "unto other gods,
but unto the Lord," 2 Kings 5.17. In the next breath he asked for pardon
if he had to go into the house of Rimmon and "I bow myself in the house
of Rimmon." Here was no complete sanctification, but Daniel and his
three companions maintained true spirituality in the prosecution of their
high office.

Chapter 3
The Image of Gold and its Consequences

The Image of Gold, 3.1-7

This event is not dated; some suggest that Daniel was aged about 40. If images existed in the first empire, then they will also exist in the last. Then an image will be made of the fourth and last beast, Rev. 13.14,15; it will have power to speak, and will be the object of worship. The worshippers of this image will receive a mark, the name of the beast or the number of his name, 666, "the number of a man." This number 6 pervades the Scriptures; man was created on the sixth day, but so often the number is attached to evil. The height of Nebuchadnezzar's image was 60 cubits (about 90 feet) and 6 cubits broad. Six kinds of musical instruments were used at its dedication, Dan. 3.5. Goliath the giant was in excess of 6 cubits in height, 1 Sam. 17.4; his spear's head weighed 600 shekels of iron, v.7; he had 6 kinds of protective devices, vs. 5-7. In the N.T., the Greek word *anathema* (curse) occurs 6 times; so does *apostereo* (defraud), *asebeia* (ungodliness), diaphthora (corruption), *echthra* (enmity) and *kakoo* (mistreat). We do not believe that all this is coincidental!

1 The chapter opens by showing the state of mind of Nebuchadnezzar. In 2.47, he had confessed the true God; now some years later he made an image-god for worship. However elevated in status, pomp and position, this is the mind of a heathen. For Paul declared that, when they knew God, they glorified Him not as God, but changed the glory of the uncorruptible God to an image made like to corruptible man, Rom. 1.21-23. So the king made this colossal image some 90 feet tall; he might have seen such an image in Egypt on one of his previous incursions there, for the heathen heart loves to copy the works

of another heathen, as Ahaz copied the great altar that he saw in Damascus, 2 Kings 16.10. No doubt this image was made of wood and overlaid with gold. Evidently he was copying his dream-image, but with the metal gold extending from the top to the base. In other words, he wanted to maintain his own status throughout all the subsequent kingdoms, with no decline as had been prophetically interpreted and predicted. It amounts to the perpetuation of the political utopia that a leader believes himself to be initiating and maintaining.

2   Nebuchadnezzar would ensure that everyone was subject to this image. Every official in his kingdom was so subject to the king's dictatorship, that without question all would worship the golden image. And if the leaders and officials engaged in such idolatry, then the people would blindly follow; how true it is that secular and religious leaders have so often led their fellows astray. This dedication of the image was one of idolatry, contrasting so vividly with the dedication of the temple under Solomon, 2 Chron. 6.18, when Solomon realized that the heaven of heavens could not contain God — how much less the house that had been built.

3   All the officials were "gathered together," as standing before the image. The ease of the operation shows the nature of the dictatorial control that Nebuchadnezzar exercised. Crowds of all nationalities gathered around. Vast crowds were not the characteristic of primitive Christianity. Large crowds followed the Lord in the Gospels, but these quickly dispersed when they did not want the truth. In Acts 2.41 and 4.4 we read of 3,000 and 5,000 men, but such numbers do not occur again; rather, there was but a little flock with few on the narrow way. Today, crowds may flock together to view high religious leaders, though this is but similar to the deification of man. Rather, the scriptural order is that the Lord's people gather together in His name.

4,5   The herald issued a command to idolatry, and all conquered people were brought into captivity of mind and soul. The hearts of unconverted men always seem ready to accept a new god, or some new doctrine. Even the children of Israel, recently come out of Egypt, were ready to say to Aaron, "Up, make us gods," Exod. 32.1. And when the molten calf was made, they deceived themselves with the words, "These be thy gods, O Israel," v.4, and were then quite ready to offer on an altar and to engage in immoral play. Years later, king Jeroboam exhorted the newly formed northern kingdom, "behold thy gods . . . which brought thee up out of the land of Egypt," 1 Kings 12.28. So the people "went to worship," v.30, so easily had Jeroboam deceived them with the two calves of gold. In other words, to get a good hearing, proclaim idolatry and heresy — but the Lord remains unknown to such people until the judgment day.

6 At the same time, the herald issued a threat, so as to ensure complete obedience. What this threat really implied was (i) if men did worship the image, then they would ultimately be cast into the lake of fire (cf. "idolaters" in Rev. 21.8); (ii) if men did not worship the image, then they would be cast into the "burning fiery furnace." The former was for eternity, the latter in time. This herald answers typically to the future anti-Christ, the beast from the earth, the one who will cause the earth-dwellers to worship the first beast and its image, Rev. 13.12,15. As many as would not worship would be killed. The similarity between the two cases is remarkable. The herald's objective was to force all people to acknowledge Nebuchadnezzar's gods to be absolutely superior to the gods of the conquered nations. (This attitude was similar to that of Sennacherib, claiming that the gods of the nations could not effect deliverance from his hands, 2 Chron. 32.13-17.)

The "burning fiery furnace" was perhaps like a common lime-kiln. There would be a perpendicular shaft to the top for an entrance, and an opening at the bottom through which to extract the lime.

7 The statement that "all the people" fell down and worshipped applies to the majority. Nothing is stated in the verse about any more faithful Jews in captivity who would not bow down to the image. The verse shows how easy it is by threats to force men to worship a huge metal object! But without the true God, idolatry in one direction easily turns to idolatry in another. The fear of this fire turned men to the image, but the fear of eternal fire does not turn many men to Christ; the love of Christ in delivering from the wrath to come is accepted only by the minority.

Daniel's Faithful Companions, 3.8-18

8,9 The Chaldeans had lost some of their authority by reason of the special position given to these faithful young Jews. So they planned the death of three of them. The accusations made against them derived from personal envy. This was so with the priests and religious leaders who accused Jesus before Pilate, stating that He forbad the giving of tribute to Caesar, Luke 23.2; yet Pilate knew "that for envy they had delivered him," Matt. 27.18. Similarly, the Jews accused Paul before Festus, Acts 25.7; "they laid many and grievous complaints against Paul, which they could not prove."

10,11 These accusers quoted to the king what he knew already, namely his absolute decree. It was a subtle manner of approach, leading up to their accusation against the three men; cf. Dan. 6.7. They quoted the exact words of the herald. In fact the similar words in verses 5,7,10,15 sound like a set-piece, so typical of formal religion. Moreover, in verse 11 the threat is also repeated, so as to remind the dictator what had to take place.

12 We now have the accusation, following the preliminaries of the previous verses. (i) **Who**? The three high Jewish officials whom Nebuchadnezzar had elevated. Their changed names are used, to denote that they were expected to be disciples of the Babylonian gods. (ii) **What**? (a) They had not regarded Nebuchadnezzar's will, and this was the crux of the matter. All dictators expect an immediate response to their will. For believers, the will of God is paramount, as Peter said, "We ought to obey God rather than ,men," Acts 5.29. (b) It was a question of worshipping "thy gods" in the plural—not just the image but the king's Babylonian gods in general. See verse 18, where the three faithful young men use the words "thy gods . . . the golden image." (c) "The golden image" in particular was not worshipped. The same is repeated in verse 18 in a question asked by the king.

The reality of the testimony of these young men was clearly known to the accusers. Others knew exactly where they stood in relation to idolatry. Such a stand for God worked against the faithful in both O.T. and N.T. days. Thus after the conversion of the apostle Paul, the Lord said to him, "they will not receive thy testimony concerning me," Acts 22.18. This has applied to many since. A true testimony (seen and known by the world, and not hidden under a bushel) has brought trouble, accusations, martyrdom, such as in the cases of Stephen and James.

13 Nebuchadnezzar's "rage and fury" shows the flesh at its worst, this rage and fury originating because just three men would not follow the dictates of his will. And this in spite of knowing the preeminence of the true God, Dan. 2.47.

14,15 So the king posed a straightforward question to those accused; were they guilty? Similarly, both the priests and Pilate asked direct questions of the Lord: "tell us whether thou be the Christ, the Son of God," "Art thou the king of the Jews?" Matt. 26.63; 27.11. The threat, issued by the herald and by the Chaldeans, was then repeated by the king; in fact, he presented a way of life (to worship the image) and a way of death (not to worship the image). This is exactly the opposite to God's way of life and way of death; cf. Jer. 21.8,9. The dictator was really issuing a challenge to God Himself, by saying, "who is that God that shall deliver you out of my hands?" Some years previously, when the Jews had been brought into captivity, God had not delivered His people into safety — He had delivered them into the hands of the king of Babylon, who had interpreted the events as if **his** gods had brought about **his** victories! It had been "through the anger of the Lord . . . he had cast them out from his presence," 2 Kings 24.20; Jer. 27.1-11. But Nebuchadnezzar always boasted of his own achievements and victories, like Sennacherib before him, 2 Kings 19.12. Contrast the assurance of Darius, "God . . . will deliver thee," Dan. 6.16.

16 The three accused men had no anxiety in answering truthfully. Others translate this verse as "we have no need to answer thee." In other words, God will answer in His way at the appropriate time (i) by delivering them miraculously, or (ii) by other means to convince Nebuchadnezzar. Both took place!

17 They trusted in the will of God, **not knowing** the direction in which His will would be manifested. Paul too was willing to trust in his God during his missionary journeys, not always knowing in which direction the divine will would lead him.

In the case of the three faithful men, there were two possibilities. (i) There would be complete deliverance from the furnace. How this could be achieved physically would not have been evident even to the most stedfast faith. Yet their testimony was, "whom we serve," contrasting with verse 12, "they serve not thy gods." They could only give this testimony if they **really did** serve God. Today, we may talk and sing much about service, but in spite of all this, we should ask, Do we **really** serve Him? In his old age, Joshua was adamant, "as for me and my house, we will serve the Lord," Josh. 24.15. The direction of true service is unique, for one cannot serve God and mammon, one cannot serve two masters, Matt. 6.24. Service is the privilege of those who are saved, of those who have "turned to God from idols to serve the living and true God," 1 Thess. 1.9.

18 (ii) If it were not God's will for immediate physical deliverance, yet even then they would not serve the king's false gods nor the golden image. As the Lord quoted during His temptation, "him only shalt thou serve," Matt. 4.10. To achieve this on the part of the Lord's people, absolute stedfastness is needed. Thus the children of Israel were far from stedfast when the golden calf was made, Exod. 32.1-8, nor when the Lord said to them prior to the captainship of Jephthah, "ye have forsaken me, and served other gods," Jud. 10.13.

The Burning Fiery Furnace, 3.19-25

19 The fact that the king was "full of fury" that any should withstand the dictator's will shows the extent to which the flesh can go. It knows no bounds when Satan motivates a man against the true God. In Nebuchadnezzar's case, we find the cruel vengeance of the flesh; the furnace was to be heated seven times hotter than normal. It is apocryphal that the flames reached a height of 49 cubits! Men of faith had to suffer cruelty in all directions, "the violence of fire, the edge of the sword, tortured, scourgings, stoned, sawn asunder," Heb. 11.33-37.

20 These three men may have resisted the king's will, but they could not resist the "most mighty men" selected to carry out the task. The three men were bound, so as to remove the last possibility of any attempt at self-preservation. God's power in deliverance was going to be seen at its maximum height, so that Nebuchadnezzar could learn a lesson.

21   This first beast cast men into the fire; the last beast will be cast alive into the lake of fire, Rev. 19.20. The three men were dropped down the entrance shaft, knowing the truth of Isaiah 43.2, "when thou walkest through the fire, thou shalt not be burned; neither shall the flame kindle upon thee," strictly referring to the future great tribulation. Throughout the ages, it has often been the case that "all that will live godly in Christ Jesus shall suffer persecution," 2 Tim. 3.12. These three men were bound around all their clothes, so that even struggling was impossible — but the more to show up the power of God. It is similar to Israel bound in Egypt, thereby showing up the delivering power of God to the uttermost.

22   These mighty men were slain by the flames—those who commit torture will likewise suffer, in time and in eternity, Matt. 26.52; God is not unmindful of evil acts committed by man against man. Usually, those who suffered had no immediate deliverance, Heb. 11.33-40; evil men appear to get away with their deeds, but not for long, since there are now a lot of men awaiting the coming judgment of God. They will be judged "according to their works," Rev. 20.12. Our verse shows the danger of being a servant to a dictator! He leads others to abominable crime, and his servants then have no defence against God's judgment when they obey his dictates. See Romans 12.19,20.

23   This is stage (i) within the furnace—the three faithful men fell down helpless in the fire.

24   Stage (ii) immediately brings forth a question from the astonished king. He saw the opposite to what should have been: four instead of three; walking instead of bound. A man of mere natural intelligence and power cannot understand the power of God over natural circumstances. Today, natural thought rejects God's power in His own creation. The Lord rejoiced that only "babes" had any understanding of divine things—the wise and prudent remained in ignorance, Matt. 11.25.

25   The fourth had the form like "the Son of God." This was the Stone of Daniel 2.45, and the "Son of man" of 7.13. It was one of the O.T. theophanies—the manifestation of the Lord prior to His incarnation. Nebuchadnezzar knew nothing of the Son of God as true deity; to him this fourth Man was merely one of his own deities or an angel—and no wonder he was astonished since none of his own deities had appeared before in miraculous circumstances! The king's testimony in 2.47 of the One true God of gods had not registered on his mind, neither had the testimony of the three faithful men, 3.17,18.

The Effect on the King, 3.26-30

26 Even at this stage the king did not recognize the unique Person of the one most high God. To the king, He was still one of many, as Paul found in Athens, Acts 17.16-23. So the three men "came forth," through the tunnel at ground level. This is almost a type of resurrection, such as when Lazarus came forth from the grave, John 11.44. More typically, it speaks of those who will come through the great tribulation, some through resurrection, Dan. 12.1,2.

27 Then the leaders, being gathered together, "saw these men" as an open demonstration of God's power. This contrasts with the resurrection of Christ; this was **not** seen by the majority of men and their leaders, and it was a fact to be accepted by faith after His ascension. **Seeing** the results of the power of God was characteristic of the O.T., such as "your eyes have seen what I have done in Egypt," Josh. 24.7.

These men walked out of the furnace, unlike Jude 23, where believers are exhorted to save others, "pulling them out of the fire." Having walked out, they were found to have their hair unsinged. How true it is that "the very hairs of your head are all numbered," Luke 12.7; the protection is divine, and even the least and the many parts are not forgotten by God. The smell of smoke clings to one's body and clothes, as is demonstrated when one passes through the smoke of a bonfire, or when one has to be in a room where the unsanctified are smoking. But here the three men are completely uncontaminated; they emerge as fresh and healthy as when they were thrown in.

28 Even to the king there was no explanation except a miraculous one. Yet he still refused to recognize the uniqueness of God. He still called them by the heathen names that reflected Nebuchadnezzar's deities. He interpreted the "Son of man" to be an angel. At least he acknowledged that God had "delivered his servants that trusted in him." Divine deliverance is a full subject in the Scriptures. For example, "Deliver the poor and needy: rid them out of the hand of the wicked," Psa. 82.4; "Jesus Christ, who gave himself for our sins, that he might deliver us from this present evil world," Gal. 1.4; "the Lord knoweth how to deliver the godly out of temptation," 2 Pet. 2.9. But for Babylon, it is stated, "they shall not deliver themselves from the power of the flame," Isa. 47.14.

These faithful men had "yielded their bodies," as should believers today, yielding them as an acceptable sacrifice to God, Rom. 12.1. By this means they "changed the king's word." In other words, the king now rescinded his threats— an absolute dictator can change his mind, because of God's intervention. This was like Pharaoh's mind at the final plague when he let Israel go. But the last beast, Dan. 7.25; Rev. 13.1, will never change his word for the better; rather it will be for the worse when he breaks his covenant in the middle of the last week, Dan. 8.27. In spite of this, the king was not wholly "converted."

29   However, Nebuchadnezzar finally made a limited confession, by insisting upon the delivering power of "the God of Shadrach, Meshach, and Abed-nego," using the idolatrous names of the three men. He did not confess that God was his God, although he recognized His superiority. If any spoke against this God (still retaining their own gods, of course) their houses would be destroyed; see our remarks on Daniel 2.5. The idea of having God and gods was often prevalent. After the Assyrians had overrun the northern kingdom of Israel, the people "feared the Lord, and made unto themselves of the lowest of them priests of the high places . . . . They feared the Lord, and served their own gods," 2 Kings 17.32,33. At the same time, the people of Judah confess-ed, "O Lord our God, other lords beside thee have had dominion over us," Isa. 26.13. Christians likewise can seek to serve God and mammon!

30   There were additional honours now available for these three faithful men; cf. 2.49. If this comes one's way without seeking a position in high places, then use it honestly. If a high position does not come one's way, then one's reward is in a far better heavenly country.

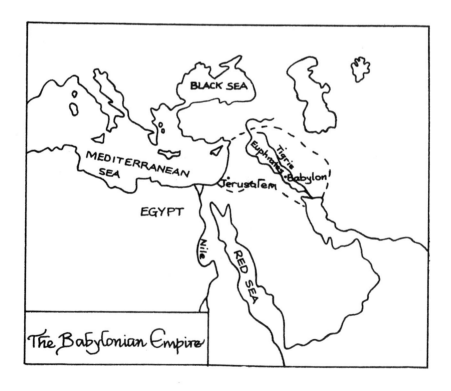

The Babylonian Empire

Chapter 4
Nebuchadnezzar's Vision of the Tree

This event is not dated in the book of Daniel, but if it occurred towards the end of the reign of Nebuchadnezzar, then Daniel would have been in captivity for about 40 years. The king had to be brought low before God and men, so as to recognize God in a fuller measure than in chapters 2 and 3. He had to be stripped of his own self-glory. Verses 1 to 3 represent the king's *own* summary of the results of the historical recollections given in verses 4-37. All are in the *first person*, except verses 28-33 (but see verse 19), where the worst experiences of all are written by the inspired historian *about* Nebuchadnezzar in the *third person*. No experience like this will be granted to the last beast, Rev. 13.1-8.

1   These words recorded by the inspired historian are not the words of God but of the king, so "all" the earth must be understood from Nebuchadnezzar's point of view: he addressed himself to his own dominions and no doubt to others that he could have captured had it been his will. His proposal of "peace" sounds like the opening of Paul's Epistles. It suggests that the king's adventurism was over, and the terrified nations need fear him no longer, since he knew of a divine Ruler far superior to himself.

2   The king thought it necessary to promulgate the news of the "signs and wonders" that a special divine intervention had accomplished in him. He referred to God's work that had abased him for seven years—he was speaking *after* the end of these seven years. There are two kinds of signs and wonders in Scripture. (i) Those referring to God's work, as "the signs and the wonders" which the Lord sent Moses to do in Egypt, Deut. 34.11; the "miracles and wonders and signs" that God did by Jesus of Nazareth, Acts 2.22. (ii) Those referring to Satan's work, through the anti-Christ for example, "the working of Satan with all power and signs and lying wonders," 2 Thess. 2.9.

3   The ultimate lesson learned was that it was "his" signs, "his" wonders," "his kingdom," "an everlasting kingdom." Personal lessons were connected with the realization that "the most High ruleth in

the kingdoms of men," vs. 17,25,32. Yet at the end of this experience, self was still present; he used the possessive "my" six times and "me" four times in verse 36. However, he could see a wider aspect of God's kingdom, which would be "from generation to generation," v.34. But the apostle Paul had learned the ultimate lesson, with self obliterated completely, writing, "I am crucified with Christ . . . Christ liveth in me," Gal. 2.20; Phil. 3.7-9.

Nebuchadnezzar's Dream of the Tree, 4.4-18

4   This verse commences the king's account of the historical events over eight years previously. He did not provide details of the dream immediately, though he visualized himself as a tree, green, prosperous and fruitful, Psa. 52.8; Luke 23.31. As "at rest" and "flourishing in my palace," the king presented his original self-satisfied boasting as an absolute dictator for whom everything was going well. Evil kings are usually like this; for example, Herod, Agrippa, Nero in the N.T. Power goes to the head of those who wield it absolutely. But ultimately, the Lord will put down all authority and power, when all enemies will be placed under His feet, 1 Cor. 15.24.

5   It is difficult to distinguish between a vision and a dream. The latter occurs during sleep, sometimes being an extension of one's personal thoughts, though the former may not occur during sleep when the vision represents something outside of oneself. The latter refers to the totality of what is perceived, but the former particularly to sight. Certainly the king had not learned the lesson of the *past* in chapter 2, that God gives dreams, and that He had a servant able to interpret them. Certainly we must derive *present* benefits from God's past dealings with us. The past must not be overlooked, for what God does in mercy once He can repeat in our experiences.

6   The king repeated what he had done years before in 2.2; he had first trusted in the devices of his wise men. He did not even remember that "God is . . . a revealer of secrets," 2.47, nor his own personal testimony in 3.28,29.

7   These wise men did not dare resort to the "tricks of the trade," for the king would not have been satisfied, so they remained silent. Today, this is a good policy—if you do not know, then do not guess or invent. Rather, we have the means of finding out apparent secrets by means of the Scriptures of truth. In the Gospels, when the apostles wanted to know, they asked the Lord who always answered suitably.

8   Daniel, the chief of the wise men, came in last. The king still thought that Daniel was mixed up with his own heathen gods, in spite of Daniel's testimony concerning his God. (i) The king addressed

Daniel by the heathen name given him previously, "according to the name of my god." For Daniel means "God is judge," but Belteshazzar means "Bel's treasure, or Bel protects the king." (ii) Daniel was the one "in whom is the spirit of the holy gods," so the king mixed the true God with his false gods. The God of gods whom Nebuchadnezzar confessed in 2.47 was superior but not unique in his estimation.

9 Again unlike 2.47, the king now refused to be clear regarding Daniel's ability to interpret the secrets of dreams, and he attributed it to "the spirit of the holy gods." He recognized Daniel's ability from his past experience in chapter 2, though this time he did not demand that the dream itself be described to him.

10 In his exposition of what had happened eight years previously, the king first told the dream, and later the interpretation was given. The tree represented Nebuchadnezzar personally. "In the midst of the earth" showed the king's pre-eminence amongst his conquered states. Its height being "great" showed his dictatorial status and authority. The image in 2.31 was also "great," but only its head represented Nebuchadnezzar; here, the whole tree represented the king, and reflected upon his pride and boasting, as in 4.30.

11 The growth of the tree showed Nebuchadnezzar's acquisition of power over the nations around—he did not inherit this, but he had to acquire it by warfare. His personal assessment of himself was that his status reached as high as heaven (like the intentions of the builders of the tower of Babel, Gen. 11.4); his estimate of himself was that of a deity on earth. This pre-eminence would reach "to the end of all the earth" —that is how he visualized the extent of his kingdom. In fact, he was abrogating to himself the very characteristics of the Lord Jesus in His future millennial reign, when His heavenly kingdom will reach throughout the whole world.

12 Trees are often used in the O.T. to describe kingdoms or rulers. Thus the vine was used for Jerusalem as fit only for burning and not for constructional purposes, Ezek. 15.2-6. In Ezekiel 17.3,12 the cedar speaks of Jerusalem and its king being led into captivity. In 31.3-9, Assyria is like a cedar exalted in height, with long branches occupied by the fowls' nests; the branches and fowls would be ruined, v.13. These were metaphors from God used by the prophet Ezekiel, but in Nebuchadnezzar's case, the metaphors were very real in his dream.

The "beasts" would denote the subjugated nations, and the "fowls" the widespread elevated authority reaching out from Babylon.

13 The "watcher and an holy one" would be an angel watching over the affairs of men. Later we read of Gabriel, 8.16; 9.21, and Michael, 10.13; 12.1, involved in Jewish and national affairs, while in the N.T. there are angels who minister to the heirs of salvation, Heb. 1.14.

No doubt originally the king associated this "watcher" with his Babylonian religion, though afterwards he knew better that the watcher was associated with "the most High," Dan. 4.17.

14   The watcher announced the dissolution of the whole system comprised of the tree, branches, beasts and fowls. This reflects upon what would happen to the Babylonian empire, later brought about by Cyrus. But primarily it refers to the downfall of Nebuchadnezzar. The axe is laid to the root of the trees, which are hewn down if no fruit is produced, Matt. 3.10. What would happen to the king would also happen to the empire afterwards. In his period of insanity, he could no longer exercise any authority, and after the empire was dissolved, no Babylonian authority would remain.

15   But the stump was to remain—Nebuchadnezzar personally would rise again after his fall. Similarly, the empire would disappear, yet the individual nations would not cease to be, for they would be taken over by the Medo-Persians. (It is the same with the image in chapter 2, and the beasts in chapter 7; the silver and the bear remain when the gold and lion pass away.) The "band of iron and brass" implied bondage, Deut. 28.48. Some suggest that the band was to keep the stump from splitting and dying, so that it could shoot again. The head of gold was being bound by the metallic character of the last two kingdoms of the dream-image of chapter 2. The wet stump was to be left with the beasts—the eagle's wings were plucked, 7.4.

16   The mental pictures of the dream now changed so as to involve a man and his changed heart. The coming insane period of the king is described. The "heart" would imply the intellect, to be changed into a form lower than that of base nature. The king would not be insane in the ordinary sense of the word, but the mental and physical state of the man would be the result of God's judgment, reducing the king to the level of his gods. As the heathen man "changed the glory of the uncorruptible God into an image made like to corruptible man, and to birds, and fourfooted beasts," Rom. 1.23, so God gave the king up to an animal-like state. This state would last for "seven times" or seven years. This period is also mentioned in verses 23,25,32. The fact that "a time" means one year is seen in Revelation, where we read of the identity of "forty and two months," 11.2; "a thousand two hundred and threescore days," 12.6; "a time, and times, and half a time," 12.14.

17   The "watchers" now occur in the plural. Moreover, the effect is to be on "the living," a word also in the plural. In other words, men were to learn by the experience of one man, the king. These watchers and holy ones appear to form a heavenly court, moving according to the will of God. Compare this with what the prophet Micaiah saw: "*all the host of heaven* standing by him (the Lord)," 1 Kings 22.19,

waiting to do His will. Various of the angelic groups in the book of Revelation, waiting to intervene on earth, may be groups of watchers.

The objective of this intervention by angels was that the king and the living should understand the dictates of divine authority that gave human authority to men of His choice. Such men were Pharaoh, Moses, Saul, David, some using their authority to rule for God, and others using their authority to act contrary to God's will. Indeed it is true that "the powers that be are ordained of God," Rom. 13.1. Often the "basest of men" are set up in positions of power; Nebuchadnezzar was one, and Pharaoh had been raised up by God so as to show His power in him, Rom. 9.17. Pilate was another, "Thou couldest have no power at all against me, except it were given thee from above," John 19.11. In fact, rulers who act as big dictators have their reward now in this present life; none ever stands the test of time.

18 Still recalling the history of eight years previously, the king recognized that Daniel was different. The fact that "the spirit of the holy gods" was in Belteshazzar (according to the king) indicates Nebuchadnezzar's idea of a multiplicity of deities. No doubt he thought the watcher and holy one in verse 13 applied to one of these. But he had a great lesson to learn; the dream by itself was not sufficient to convey this lesson, neither was the following interpretation. Only the seven-year experience would suffice to teach the king God's lesson.

Daniel's Interpretation of the Dream, 4.19-27

Although Nebuchadnezzar had been relating past history in the first person since verse 4, the narrative now reverts to the third person and this is particularly noticeable in verses 28-33 where the actual accomplishment of the dream is described. No doubt it was too awkward for the king to relate this directly to his subjects, so someone else acted as spokesman for the king, to whom he had previously related the details.

19 Daniel was troubled, and hesitated for one hour to inform the king of the meaning of the dream, since it was something so terrible and referred to the head of gold. Apart from this hour, there is no gap between verses 18 and 19, unlike between 2.13 and 2.14 where a whole night intervened. Hence it appears that God gave the interpretation to Daniel immediately. The king tried to raise Daniel above his obvious confusion. But Daniel commenced with a very tactful opening statement: If only the dream applied to the king's enemies! No such tact was necessary when the Lord was confronted with those who hated Him; He said directly, "Ye are of your father the devil," John 8.44.

20,21 Daniel first gave a long description of the dream (repeating verses 11 and 12), obviously to delay coming to the point. The king allowed this, unlike 2.8 where he sensed impotence on behalf of his wise men.

22   The climax was reached when Daniel said, "It is *thou.*" This contrasts with 2.38, "*Thou* art this head of gold." Other examples of such a personal climax are, "*Thou* art the man" spoken by Nathan to David, 2 Sam. 12.7, and "*Thou* hast said" spoken by the Lord to Judas, Matt. 26.25. Nebuchadnezzar had "grown" from humble beginnings; he had "become strong," his military strength being superior to that of all nations; his greatness "reacheth unto heaven," and this suggests his pride *reaching up* as an obnoxious thing to God's throne; "thy dominion to the end of the earth" implies his victories *sideways* over all the surrounding nations.

23   This repeats verses 13-16, so as to make quite sure that Nebuchadnezzar would realize that the interpretation rested exactly on the details of the dream, and was not being manufactured by Daniel.

24   The decree came from "the most High," from the great Judge at the court of heaven, who was directing His angels in their work of judgment. It is indeed "a fearful thing to fall into the hands of the living God," Heb. 10.31. As an example of this angelic work, we may mention the case of Herod when he was acclaimed as a god — "immediately the angel of the Lord smote him," Acts 12.23.

25   Daniel stated what would become of the king for seven years. He would be driven from men—from his palace, his position and his power. He would be with the beasts of the field—perhaps in an animal reserve in the fields of his palace away from the gaze of men. He would be made like that to which he had reduced the living God. He would eat grass, unlike the splendid court food alluded to in 1.5 and 5.1. He would be wet with the dew of heaven, no doubt like the "Legion" always in the mountains and tombs, Mark 5.5. This insane state would be necessary for *seven* years so that he could learn of the authority of God; compare this with the *three* years of Daniel's schooling in chapter 1. This insane state of the head of gold and of the first beast is in complete contrast with the Stone and the Son of man, namely with the Lord Jesus as King. He shall dwell amongst His own, and the throne of the Lamb shall be in the holy city, new Jerusalem, Rev. 22.3. Then "a little child" shall lead the wolf, the lamb, the leopard, the kid, the calf and the lion, Isa. 11.6-8.

26   Yet the promise was made: at the end of the seven years "thy kingdom shall be sure unto thee." Nebuchadnezzar would survive, and the golden kingdom would continue to exist. The phrase "after that" is important. In other words, the solemn seven-year lesson *would be learned*, quite unlike Pharaoh's case since he did not learn the lesson of God's mighty hand, Exod. 3.19. Of course, God's foreknowledge of such events did not force any man into his line of action; men are always responsible. For example, "one of you shall betray me" and "Thou shalt deny me thrice"; the Lord knew, but Judas and Peter were responsible.

The lesson learned would be "the heavens do rule"; namely, there would be no throne in Jerusalem. During the times of the Gentiles, God rules from heaven amongst the nations.

27 Yet Daniel held out a way of escape. His counsel being acceptable reminds us of Paul's words, "now is the accepted time
. . . now is the day of salvation," 2 Cor. 6.2. All the king had to do was to break off his pride, cruelty, idolatry, his subjugation of the poor and his murderous activity. Daniel meant that the king had to bring forth works meet for repentance; the works of faith as a N.T. concept were, of course, absent. Rather it would seem to be a case of Romans 2.8-10, "un-to them that . . . do not obey the truth, but obey unrighteousness, in-dignation and wrath, tribulation and anguish, upon every soul of man that doeth evil, of the Jew first, and also of the Gentile; but glory, honour, and peace, to every man that worketh good, to the Jew first, and also to the Gentile." If there were repentance, there would be "a lengthening of thy tranquility," or peace. This would last to the end of his physical life, based on the righteousness of the law and not of faith; it cannot refer to eternal life when no real faith is present.

Additionally, his repentance had to bring forth "mercy to the poor." Evidently this dictator had had no mercy on the poor, as his kingdom had been built up on cruelty and oppression. The position of faith has been declared by the Lord, by the prophets and apostles, "that we should remember the poor," Gal. 2.10; Rom. 15.26; "do good unto all men, especially unto them who are of the household of faith," Gal. 6.10.

Fulfilment and Restoration, 4.28-37

The historical fulfilment in verses 28-33 is recorded in the *third person* —a spokesman held forth in place of the king, no doubt because this part was too bad for the king to expound! After verse 34, the narrative returns to the *first person* —the king's own words.

28 It all happened as had been interpreted in the dream. Compare
this with Genesis 41.54, "the seven years of dearth began to come, *according as* Joseph had said."

29 After one year of having received the warning, Nebuchadnezzar
walked "on" his palace, for the gardens were above. He was allowed twelve months to repent, but he would not. Elsewhere, the Lord had said, "and ye would not," Matt. 23.37; see Isa. 30.15. The church at Thyatira was given "space to repent," and "she repented not," Rev. 2.21.

30 Upon looking round, the king burst forth with pride of self-
achievement—"my power, my majesty." Perhaps even the Lord's people can think that way sometimes; for example, the apostles "told him all that *they* had done," Luke 9.10. It is the spirit of self-glory,

as in Herod's case when "he gave not God the glory," Acts 12.23. It was pretension that had built the first Babylon, Gen. 11.4-6; it will be religious pretension that adorns the future Babylon, "How much she hath glorified herself . . . I sit as queen," Rev. 18.7. And so it was with Nebuchadnezzar; he had built "this great Babylon" —how? "By the might of my power," no doubt using slave labour. Contrast this with Solomon's rehearsal of what he had built, 2 Chron. 6.2,10,18. And why was Babylon built? —for "the honour of *my* majesty." How this contrasts with the Lord; He sought not His own glory, but possessed eternal intrinsic glory; He was given glory, and glory is ascribed to Him by worshippers.

31   When judgment falls, it falls swiftly; compare "this night," Luke 12.20, and "sudden destruction," 1 Thess. 5.3. The word "while" in our verse shows that the judgment fell at the very time of the king's boasting, "by thy words thou shalt be condemned," Matt. 12.37. The origin of the judgment was "from heaven," and this is also the origin of salvation: a light and a voice came "from heaven" to Saul on the Damascus road, Acts 9.3. Moreover the voice said, "O king Nebuchadnezzar"—it was to one named individual, as in John 11.43 (to Lazarus) and Acts 9.4 (to Saul). Both judgment and salvation are intensely personal matters.

The voice declared that "The kingdom is departed from thee"—a separation of the kingdom from the dictator, at least for seven years. The head of gold was removed, though the first kingdom still remained for some years. It is similar to the temporary disappearance of the fourth beast at the end of Daniel 7.7 prior to its emergence after the period known as "the gap" of the church age, for the beast "was, *and is not*; and shall ascend," Rev. 17.8.

32   This verse repeats Daniel's interpretation given in verse 25. What this means is that Daniel had been completely in touch with heaven when giving the interpretation, so its later fulfilment was exact as to detail. We, too, repeat a heavenly message previously given by inspiration, so its details must be true.

33   The fulfilment of the details of the seven years repeats verse 25 again. But there is the addition "eagles' feathers" and "nails like birds' claws." He became physically what he had been metaphorically in the years of his cruelty and conquests. (These symbols are used in 7.4 and 7.19, relating to the first and fourth beast respectively.) The full details of the seven years are passed over in silence; it is said that the king was kept in the palace fields, so that no one should see his humiliation. A speaker other than the king was rehearsing this, and quickly passed over the sad scene.

34   More pleasant matters occur in this verse, so the *first person* appears again; Nebuchadnezzar continued his personal discourse. This opportunity to confess the truth had been provided by the fact of judgment, and the king did not lose the opportunity. This is unlike the last political beast in Revelation 13-19, who will be in permanent rebellion against God. In Daniel 2.46, Nebuchadnezzar fell upon his face, but here he lifted up his eyes to heaven. Whereas the act is the same as in John 17.1, yet how different was the Son of God, who could confess that He had glorified *His Father* on the earth, v.4. Nebuchadnezzar had glorified *himself* through his life! In John 17.3, the Father's intervention from heaven had been to send the Son; in Daniel 4 the intervention had been seven years judgment upon Nebuchadnezzar.

At last the king knew (i) the most High, (ii) that He lives for ever (unlike all men and their kingdoms), (iii) that He rules for ever in "his everlasting dominion," (iv) that His kingdom passes on regardless of changes on earth.

35   As for men on earth, including himself, the king confessed that they were "nothing"; "What is man?" asked the psalmist in a different frame of mind, Psa. 8.4. The divine will is done in heaven, and also on earth, the king concluded, a truth that the Lord included in the disciples' prayer, "Thy will be done in earth, as it is in heaven," Matt. 6.10. Most leaders today, including all dictators throughout history, do not reach as far as this Gentile emperor in their understanding of the subject of divine control. No one can prevent His will being accomplished, nor can they question it directly to His face.

36   Thus Daniel at least looked for the end of the seven years, as he would be looking forward to the end of the 70 years captivity, 9.2. The king returned to his same mental and physical state as he possessed seven years previously, with the difference that he could now make this great profession. Yet pride still seemed to be present (though note what he says at the end of verse 37). It is easy to test the spirit of pride: Would the Lord Jesus have spoken like that? If not, then this shows up Nebuchadnezzar's natural pride. He spoke of "the glory of *my* kingdom"—his regained authority over his territories; "*mine* honour" —his personal status owned by men; "brightness"—his personal high-living in his palace. He was the centre of attention and reverence, and the word "added" suggests that he had even higher status than before.

37   The king's conclusion forms his last recorded words in Scripture. His testimony to all nations concerned the divine King's Person, work and ways. He seems to look forward to the finality of the future: pride leads to an abasement that has no rising again in eternity, whether for a dictator, his officers or his subjects.

Chapter 5
The Downfall of the First Kingdom

We now read of the immediate events that brought about the fall of the Babylonian kingdom. Although it is God who changes kingdoms according to His will, yet He uses the evil of the nation ripe for judgment that falls, and the hunger for conquest of the nation taking over. Nearly 70 years have passed since chapter 1, so Daniel is an old man well into his eighties, and only a few more years have to pass before the Book of Daniel draws to a close.

In chapter 5, we read of the idolatrous feasting in Belshazzar's palace, vs. 1-4, an example of "let us eat and drink; for tomorrow we die," 1 Cor. 15.32; Luke 12.19, and "before the flood they were eating and drinking . . . and knew not until the flood came, and took them all away," Matt. 24.38,39. The king must have known that the Medes and Persians were surrounding his capital city! There came the writing on the wall, and none of the king's advisers could read or interpret it, vs. 5-9, The queen then recalled Daniel's ability that had been demonstrated years before, vs. 10-12, chapters 2 and 4 showing Daniel's capacity to interpret dreams. The king expressed his personal confidence in Daniel, vs. 13-16, who reminded him how God had humbled Nebuchadnezzar, vs. 17-21, though Belshazzar was not humbled, vs. 22,23. Thus the writing was interpreted and the kingdom came promptly to its end, vs. 24-31.

The Idolatrous Feasting in the Palace, 5.1-4.

1 Here we have the heights of godless revelry, a leader making folly before 1,000 of his subjects of the highest classes. The cost of such feasting was borne no doubt by the taxes taken from the masses. In this feasting, there was no recognition of the fundamental principle that it is the God of heaven who raises the leaders up. The climax was that of abandoned drunkenness, 1 Pet. 4.3, with religious hymns to enliven the proceedings. This should be compared with Mystery Babylon

the great in Revelation 17-18, "in one hour so great riches is come to nought," 18.16,17. What a contrast to the rejoicing of the saints above, 5.8-10.

2 A new height of abomination was reached during the feast. Originally, Nebuchadnezzar had carried away to Babylon the vessels of the house of the Lord, 2 Chron. 36.7; this was 13 years before the glory of God left the temple, Ezek. 10.4; 11.23, and 20 years before the temple was destroyed. But Belshazzar's idolatrous feast took place only about two years before the return of the vessels to Jerusalem, Ezra 1.3,7,8. Such incarceration of holy things in unholy surroundings can likewise be seen when the ark of the covenant was placed in the house of Dagon, the Philistines' god, 1 Sam. 5.2, when Paul appeared in king Agrippa's court, Acts 25.23, and when the Lord appeared before the high priest and Pilate. Today, many holy N.T. institutions are used in circles of unbelief and ritual.

3 Although God had left and disowned the house in Jerusalem as far as the Jews were concerned, yet when the house is seen in relation to the Gentiles and their idolatry, it has its full name, "the temple of the house of God." For such evil, Belshazzar was about to die, later to be replaced by Cyrus the Persian who would enable the house to be rebuilt and the vessels to be returned, Isa. 44.28; Ezra 1.7.

4 The holy vessels were to be used for the base sin of drunkenness, something that formed one of the main sins of the Bible record, committed by Noah, Gen. 9.21; Nadab and Abihu, Lev. 10.1,11, and some in the Corinthian church, 1 Cor. 11.21. In Belshazzar's court, this evil went hand-in-hand with idolatry, characterized by six different kinds of materials, "gold, silver, brass, iron, wood, stone." (The first four metals being the same as in the dream-image of chapter 2 is not without its significance.) The number "six" shows the connection with the basest level of human nature, forming part of the number 666 of the final beast, Rev. 13.18. Today, materialism forms the central attraction for the hearts of men, and John would exhort his spiritual children to keep themselves from idols, 1 John 5.21; 2 Cor. 6.16.

The Writing on the Wall, 5.5-12

5 There was sudden divine intervention "in the same hour." We think similarly of the flood, of Nadab and Abihu, of Korah, of Jehoram, 2 Chron. 21.18, and of Ananias and Sapphira. In our verse, the writing represented a warning and a demonstration of God's power through Daniel, before the climax of judgment was reached later that night. The "fingers" were visible to the king. God was thereby using anthropomorphic means with which to communicate with an evil man.

We think of His writing on the tables of stone on mount Sinai, Exod. 31.18; 32.16; 34.28; Deut. 10.2,4, and of the Lord's writing on the ground, John 8.6. In both cases the "finger" is mentioned. In heaven, the names of God's people are written in the Lamb's book of life—would this be by the divine finger?; if God could blot out names then He could also write, Exod. 32.33.

6 Those at the feast immediately experienced fear at such an unusual divine intervention, for it is a fearful thing to fall into the hands of the living God, Heb. 10.31. The Lord's people also experienced fear before the manifestation of God. Moses said, "I exceedingly fear and quake," Heb. 12.21, while John "fell at his feet as dead," Rev. 1.17.

7 The immediate recourse of the king was in his astrologers, thereby following the custom of Nebuchadnezzar before him, Dan. 2.2. Belshazzar wanted to know two things, (i) the reading of the writing, and (ii) its interpretation. Evidently the writing was not in a form that was immediately recognizable as words. As the Lord Jesus said later, "thou hast hid these things from the wise and prudent," Matt. 11.25, and as Paul wrote, "the things of God knoweth no man," 1 Cor. 2.11. There is a case worse than that of Belshazzar: the Pharisees thought that they could see, and so were blind, John 9. 39-41.

If anyone could read the symbolism on the wall, and interpret it, then the highest reward in the land would be his—a status that could only be given by an absolute monarch. Pharaoh had done this previously when Joseph had interpreted the two dreams, Gen. 41.42,43. But there is a difference between the two cases: in Daniel, the promise of reward was made *before* anyone interpreted the dream, but in Pharaoh's case no promise had been made beforehand.

8 The wise men exhibited complete ignorance, and rightly so! They had no desire to guess. It is the same today; most men understand nothing of the prophetic message in Scripture, though the "experts" are willing to theorize and to go into print.

9 The king's last resource had failed, as had the broken cisterns, Jer. 2.13, and the arm of the flesh, 2 Chron. 32.8; Jer. 17.5. The verse shows how much the king relied on these methods of the flesh. and when they failed, the king crumpled up.

10 The "queen" would no doubt be the queen-mother, for the king's wives were already present at the feast, v.2. This queen remembered Daniel, who had perhaps been deposed after the death of Nebuchadnezzar, and had later been forgotten by subsequent kings and by Belshazzar. Daniel had not been included amongst "all the king's wise men," v.8. The queen's aspirations did not fit in with the gravity of the situation. Her form of greeting and comfort, "O king, live for ever," was

far from fact (of course unknown to her), but Belshazzar would be slain that night.

11   The queen provided a glowing testimony of Daniel as a man of God of previous years, though her words about Daniel were coloured by her idolatry when she said, "in whom is the spirit of the holy gods" and "like the wisdom of the gods." Men likewise falsely accused the Lord, associating wrong religious ideas with His life, such as casting out devils through Beelzebub the prince of the devils, Matt. 12.24.

Daniel had "light and understanding and wisdom," and this is how a Christian should appear before the world, even if the world fails to understand the origin of these features. For example, the men who disputed with Stephen were not able to resist "the wisdom and the spirit by which he spake," Acts 6.10; see 1 Cor. 12.8. Moreover, Daniel had been made "master" of the Chaldean system, although as a man of God he could not have imbibed anything from it. In other words, even if a Christian is raised to high office, he nevertheless remains separate from any deeds that are not consistent with the Christian profession. There are many things in the commercial, legal, educational, political and religious circles of men's organizing that a Christian cannot touch: "Come out of her, my people, that ye be not partaker of her sins," Rev. 18.4; 2 Cor. 6.17. The taking of this attitude and position will mark out a Christian more and more, and men will think it strange that "ye run not with them to the same excess of riot," 1 Pet. 4.4.

12   The queen's testimony was that Daniel excelled above all others—because his gifts were from God, 1.17. It appears that Daniel gave sound counsel in many different walks of life. The queen associated this with the heathen name Belteshazzar (Bel's treasure, or Bel protects the king), but this concept was not going to be any good in protecting the king that night! She also used the proper name of Daniel (God is judge), and that is exactly what God was about to do.

Compare the queen's testimony with that of the butler to Pharaoh concerning Joseph, Gen. 41.9-13. He was called to Pharaoh to interpret his two dreams regarding the seven kine and the seven ears of corn, for in that case also, none of the magicians and wise men of Egypt could interpret the dream.

Daniel before Belshazzar, 5.13-23

13   While the armies of the Medes and the Persians were about to invade Babylon, Daniel appeared before the king, who unwittingly used the prophet's name "Daniel," declaring in ignorance what God was about to do. He recalled events nearly 66 years previously, when the Jewish captivity commenced. He thought of the beginning of the "head of gold," but Daniel would speak of its end.

14   The king merely quoted the testimony of the queen—they were
      not words out of his own experience. It appears that Belshazzar
had not heard of Daniel, who seems to have lost his authority when
Nebuchadnezzar died. What the king *did know* is stated in verse 22,
namely the period of insanity of Nebuchadnezzar years before.

15   Belshazzar readily confessed the failure of his own men. This
      failure always followed a message from God that had to be inter-
preted, for the natural man does not understand the things of the Spirit
of God, 1 Cor. 2.14, for "they are spiritually discerned." Hence we must
beware of the theological utterances of unbelieving men, and of transla-
tions of the Scriptures by unbelieving scholars.

16   Again he said, "I have heard," quoting the queen's words. The
      definite promise was made—Daniel would have status and
power. Of course Daniel disclaimed them in verse 17, but accepted them
in verse 29 because this was in keeping with God's will. "The third ruler"
means that Daniel would stand third in the chain of command under
Belshazzar and another man. In God's plan, this enabled Daniel to have
high office at the beginning of the next kingdom, 6.2. Compare this with
Joseph who rode in the second chariot, and who was ruler over all Egypt,
Gen. 41.42,43. But contrast this with the Lord's case; when men wanted
to make Him king by force, He refused, until God sets Him as King on
the holy hill of Zion, Psa. 2.6-9.

17   Daniel's response prior to his interpretation of the writing is
      given in verses 17-23. He had no desire to receive any reward
from the world for doing the service of God; when he made these
remarks he must have known that Belshazzar was about to die. Similarly, Peter would accept no money when Simon of Samaria offered it,
Acts 8.20, neither would Elisha even though Naaman urged him to take
it, 2 Kings 5.16. But it would not be wrong to accept something from the
world where natural love and charity form the motive, as for example in
Acts 28.10 where the men of Melita "laded us with such things as were
necessary" because of Paul having healed many diseases.

18   Daniel dwelt on the past; the lesson from Nebuchadnezzar, vs.
      18-21, is applied to Belshazzar, vs. 22,23. The prophet recalled
that Nebuchadnezzar's supreme authority derived from God: "the God
of heaven hath given thee a kingdom," 2.37; "the most High . . . giveth
it (the kingdom) to whomsoever he will," 4.25. Of course, many powerful dictators have never realized this great truth!, and they use this power
entirely for their own ends.

19   The relationship between Nebuchadnezzar and his peoples is
      then described. (i) They "trembled and feared," but not before
God. (ii) The very life of men was in his hands—he killed or kept alive
whom he would. This power was from God; its use was Satanic. Com-

pare Pilate's case, "Thou couldest have no power at all against me, except it were given thee from above," John 19.11. The use of this power by Nebuchadnezzar is seen in Daniel 3 against Daniel's three friends. (iii) National status was granted or removed. This is seen in Daniel 2.48,49. Pharaoh elevated the butler and Joseph, but he removed the baker from office by prison and death.

20 Daniel now recalled chapter 4, events that took place many years previously. God too raises up, and also abases, a thought that entered the teaching of the Lord Jesus Christ several times. In verse 18, God raised up, though using various human channels to achieve it. Here in verse 20 God reversed this, using "they" as human channels to effect it. Compare this with Job 1.21, "the Lord gave, and the Lord hath taken away."

21 Daniel recalled the seven years' insanity of Nebuchadnezzar, events that he had interpreted from the tree-dream years before. That king had sunk to the lowest level in status and activity, until the lesson had been learned in the hard way. Most dictators never learn that the most High rules in the kingdom of men, setting over it men whom He chooses, since "there is no power but of God," Rom. 13.1. But God insisted that the first dictator would learn the lesson. In fact, God insisted upon a lot of first lessons — whatever happened afterwards. For example, Nadab and Abihu in the beginning of the tabernacle era, Lev. 10.1-3, and Ananias and Sapphira in the beginning of the church era, Acts 5.1-11.

22 This past event should have been a lesson to subsequent kings, but Belshazzar took no heed. We are responsible to learn from God's past dealings with men: the knowledge of the Scriptures should produce its own fruit to correction and instruction, 2 Tim. 3.16.

23 Many would lift up themselves against the Lord—deliberate rebellion against His absolute authority. Daniel recalled the infamous sin of that night—the idolatrous use of the vessels from the Lord's house in Jerusalem. How did Daniel know about these vessels and Belshazzar's use of them? Had he seen them as he entered, or had God given him that knowledge? At least, God knew! Compare Ezekiel 8.5-16, where God showed Ezekiel what He knew, and Revelation 2-3, where the Lord showed John what He knew. Moreover, the king had shared his idolatrous feast with many others, worshipping idol gods that possessed no mental powers; "They have mouths, but they speak not: eyes have they, but they see not . . . ," Psa. 115.4-7; 135.15-17; in the case of Baal, "there was no voice, nor any that answered," 1 Kings 18.26,29. Such rebellion was against the One "in whose hand thy breath is" —Daniel's warning that the end had come, when God would take away from the king the very basis of life. Such rebellion meant that the king had not glorified God. This is like the case of Herod, Acts 12.23, contrasting with the responsibility of believers in body and spirit, 1 Cor. 6.20, and with the perfect life of the Lord Jesus when on earth, John 17.4.

The Interpretation and Fulfilment, 5.24-31

24 With all this condemnation having been given, Daniel showed that the hand manifested deity prepared for an act of immediate judgment. The change in the kingdom was wrought by God as an act of judgment. A deed far worse than Nebuchadnezzar's pride needed judgment of a far greater duration than the seven years' insanity. And there was to be no recovery, neither of the king nor of the nation, Jer. 51.60-64.

25 Daniel could read the words of the writing, but we are not told why the Chaldeans could not. The Aramaic writing consisted only of the consonants with no vowels, namely "mn mn tql prs." The addition of different vowels in enunciating this would provide different groups of words, none of which conveyed any meaning or implication as a whole to the wise men. Divinely helped, Daniel read the words as *"mene, mene, tekel, upharsin,"* namely, "numbered, numbered, weighed, divided," and he then applied these words to Belshazzar.

26 *Mene*: In God's purpose, the Babylonian kingdom had a determined span of existence, and its end had come. As Paul said in Athens, "God . . . hath determined the times before appointed, and the bounds of their habitation," Acts 17.26. No doubt this can be said about all kingdoms that have arisen and fallen in past history (whatever the *natural* means used by God for their overthrow). The repetition of the word *mene* adds to its importance and urgency, and the reader may care to recall many other duplicated names in both O.T. and N.T.

27 *Tekel*: The life and policy of Belshazzar were weighed and found completely deficient when contrasted with the will of God. The thought of God weighing is found in other passages. "By him actions are weighed," said Hannah, 1 Sam. 2.3; "All the ways of a man are clean in his own eyes; but the Lord weigheth the spirits," wrote Solomon, Prov. 16.2, and "A just weight and balance are the Lord's," v.11; "thou, most upright, dost weigh the path of the just," Isa. 26.7. These weights are spelled out in "the books," which will be opened for judgment before the great white throne, Rev. 20.12.

28 *Peres*: The word *upharsin* on the wall means "and divided" in the plural. When Daniel said *peres*, he dropped the *u* meaning "and", and changed the verb to the singular, so as to apply it to Belshazzar particularly. The consonants "prs" can also be given vowels to form the word "Persians", so Daniel could extract *two* thoughts from this consonant-group — the division of the Babylonian kingdom between the united nations of the Medes and the Persians.

29 Did Belshazzar and his one thousand lords believe the message? No doubt they thought that Babylon was impregnable. But nevertheless, glory and a superior status were given to Daniel, who carried this new position of authority into the kingdom following, 6.2. Today, men do not believe what the Scriptures say about the end of the kingdoms of men, nor that the night of darkness is far spent, Rom. 13.12. Politicians perceive an ultimate utopia gained by mutual agreements between nations gradually displacing warfare and introducing an era of peace; theologians see this utopia being formed by the spread of *their* gospel—human love without the sacrificial blood of Christ.

30,31 So Belshazzar was slain that night, and he had no time for repentance. He lost the opportunity at the last minute, while the thief on the cross gained it at the last minute.

How was this overthrow achieved? The armies of Cyrus surrounded Babylon. Some books are very extravagant in their description of the fortifications of Babylon, but others are much more cautious and conservative. Some authors have written of double walls 300 feet high and 85 feet broad, Jer. 51.53,58. The city was divided by the river Euphrates; its banks were protected by walls and brass gates, and they were connected by a bridge 1,000 yards long with a palace at both ends. The palace of Belshazzar is said to have been surrounded by three sets of walls, some 300 feet high with towers higher still. But other authors state much smaller figures for these fortifications. Yet how did Cyrus take the city? His armies dug a new course for the river, and at the time of the feast, the old course was closed, and his men marched along the riverbed and through the palace gates. Thus God used this great army of the second kingdom to judge Babylon. He will also use the future armies of the fourth beast to destroy the religious Babylon of the coming day, Rev. 17.16. But God Himself will judge directly the fourth beast and the false prophet (the anti-Christ), 19.20. Thus Belshazzar had a pound of responsibility, and in judgment this was entirely taken away, Luke 19.24,26.

Note that there were two kings named Darius. (i) "Darius the Median" in our verse 31, who reigned **before** Cyrus. (ii) "Darius king of Persia," Ezra 4.24; 5.6; 6.1, some 17 years later, who reigned **after** Cyrus.

Chapter 6
Daniel Condemned to the Den of Lions

In just the same way as there was faithfulness at the beginning of the first kingdom, Dan. chs. 1-3, so too at the beginning of the second kingdom. All these records will give encouragement to any who pass through persecution and in particular through the great tribulation of the end times. In chapter 6, Daniel was given the very highest status in the kingdom, although by then he was very old, vs. 1-3. There were 102 other leaders who were very jealous of Daniel, so they plotted against him, getting Darius unwittingly to sign a decree that there was to be no prayer except through the king as deified, vs. 4-9. Yet Daniel prayed as before, vs. 10,11, so the 122 men accused Daniel before the king, insisting that he be cast into the den of lions. Too late Darius realized the trap into which he had fallen. Not being an absolute dictator, he could not reverse the decree, vs. 12-15. Daniel was miraculously delivered by God, even after he had been cast into the den, vs. 16-24; Darius then issued a second decree that all were to fear before the God of Daniel, vs. 25-28.

The Plot against Daniel, 6.1-9

1   The Persian empire was divided into provinces—seventeen years later there were 127 provinces, Esther 1.1. In Daniel 6.1 we conclude that there were 120 provinces, each administered by a prince, or a satrap. Even though it "pleased Darius" to make these arrangements, yet God was behind the choice, since the powers that be are ordained of God, Rom. 13.1.

2   Additionally, there were three "presidents," to ensure that the satraps obtained the right taxes for the king. These satraps gave accounts to the presidents, so that the king should suffer no loss financially.

3   As an old man of mature years, Daniel was the first president. He had "an excellent spirit," a result of 70 years faithfulness towards God. The honour conferred upon him by Belshazzar in Daniel 5.29 was carried over into the second kingdom. The relationship between

honesty in the things of the world and faithfulness in the things of God is seen in Luke 16.10-12. The two go together, "He that is faithful in that which is least is faithful also in much," 16.10. Hence the record of the faithfulness of Daniel continues to the end of the chapter.

4   The 120 satraps and two presidents were jealous that a captive Jew had the top job! So they all sought to discredit him as regards his administration in the kingdom. Most of these 122 were dishonest, as were the publicans (the taxgatherers) in the N.T., who had to gather taxes for the Romans. Unlike Zacchaeus, Luke 19.8, there was no "error or fault" in Daniel, a sure lesson concerning the necessity of absolute honesty in the Christian's employment.

5   Therefore they had to seek trickery pertaining to Daniel's true religion, to the law of his God. This is what men sought to do against Paul, claiming that he was "a mover of sedition among all the Jews," while Paul responded with the assertion that they could not prove any of these accusations, Acts 24.5,13. Other kinds of trickery were adopted against the Lord Jesus; they asked Him so-called difficult questions, Matt. 22.15-33, and at the same time they "sent forth spies, which should feign themselves just men, that they might take hold of his words, that so they might deliver him unto the power and authority of the governor," Luke 20.20.

6   Hence these men would use the regularity of Daniel's prayers to his God, but not to their gods. The two presidents and the 120 satraps plotted together to suggest to Darius that **all** were agreed (seemingly including Daniel). If any misrepresent the Christian's faith, the exhortation must be: remain faithful. The men addressed Darius by "live for ever," though shortly afterwards Cyrus became king. It shows the lack of meaning in such hollow sentiments, as in 5.10.

7   The Persian kings were regarded as representations of the gods (like the popes over the centuries), and can be regarded now as typical of the anti-Christ. Thus it would seem reasonable for all the captured nations to approach their gods only through Darius, else any offender would be cast into the den of lions, which were half-starved. (This is a Satanic pre-copy of Christians, who approach the Father on high through the Lord Jesus who once became flesh.)

8   As soon as the king had signed this decree, the law was binding, and could not be changed. The conspirators knew this, and used it for their own evil end. (Compare the law that could not be altered in Esther 1.19, where Vashti was deposed from being queen because of disobedience to the king's command.)

9   Flattery regarding the king's exalted status gripped the heart of king Darius, so he readily signed the decree without appreciating its significance, certainly not realizing that he had in effect signed

Daniel's death-warrant. Even from a natural point of view, a Christian must take great care when signing any document, so that he knows full well that to which he is binding himself. In Exodus 19.8, the children of Israel bound themselves to the keeping of the law, even though at that time they did not yet know its contents.

The King's Dilemma, 6.10-15

10 As the Lord Jesus was "faithful amidst unfaithfulness," so too was Daniel. Knowing all the consequences, he continued in his prayer-life as before. Being well over 80 years old, he himself had proved the power of God previously, and he also knew the power of God revealed throughout Jewish history from Abraham onwards. The lions' den therefore held no terrors for him. David had said long before Daniel's experience, "The Lord that delivered me out of the paw of the lion . . . ," 1 Sam. 17.34,37, and Paul would recount later that "I was delivered out of the mouth of the lion (emperor Nero)," 2 Tim. 4.17.

All the conspirators knew that Daniel prayed toward Jerusalem. This was not to be seen of men, but to follow the words of Solomon, "hearken thou . . . when they shall pray toward this place," 1 Kings 8.30, and "if they shall . . . make supplication unto thee in the land of them that carried them captives, saying, We have sinned . . . and pray unto thee *toward* their land . . . the city which thou has chosen, and *the house* which I have built for thy name," vs. 46-48. Both city and house had been destroyed, but the principle still applied. See also Psalm 5.7; 28.2. The kind of prayer that occupied Daniel's heart is found in Daniel 9.3-19, which we shall consider later. Certainly the prophet's praying was not like that which the Lord condemned in Matthew 6.5, where men loved to pray in the streets to be seen of men. In spite of being seen by men, Daniel's attitude of heart would be to enter his room, to shut the door, and to pray in secret, when he would be rewarded openly. Daniel did this three times a day, as David said, "Evening, and morning, and at noon, will I pray," Psa. 55.17, the Jewish "day" commencing in the evening.

11 Did the assembling of the conspirators take place on the same day as that on which the decree had been signed? So as to lose no time in achieving their plans? If men assembled against the Lord, Psa. 2.1-3, then they would also be ready to assemble themselves against a faithful disciple. In any case, they *knew* what Daniel would do—they knew the consistency of his faith. What do men know of our faith? From what Jacob said to Pharaoh in Genesis 47.9, the king would not know much about that patriarch's faith!

12 Their attitude was most subtle. They asked the king for confirmation of what he had done, to prevent any possibility of delay.

It reminds us of Daniel 3.9-11, where the Chaldeans recalled to Nebuchadnezzar the decree that he had made regarding the worship of the golden image.

13 These men proceeded to describe a saint of God in a most evil way. The attitude of men to Christians, and God's later visitation against them, also applies today: "having your conversation honest among the Gentiles: that, whereas they speak against you as evildoers, they may by your good works, which they shall behold, glorify God in the day of visitation," 1 Pet. 2.12.

They referred to Daniel as an exile from Judah, rather than as the chief of the presidents and satraps. They insinuated that he would be suspect both on political and religious grounds (not, of course, in reality, but according to their own argument). This is a common trick by some politicians to disgrace others. They interpreted Daniel's loyalty to his God as disloyalty to king Darius (this is how the Jews falsely represented the Lord Jesus before Pilate, Luke 23.2). Of course, this was not so; Daniel had his priorities right. He knew that kings were set up by God, and there must needs be submission to them, 1 Pet. 2.13,14, except when the divine claims show up any immorality in human demands. Thus Peter said, "We ought to obey God rather than men," Acts 5.29; apart from cases like this, resisting authority is equivalent to resisting the "ordinance of God," Rom. 13.2. Daniel was not like this when his prayer-life before God resisted entirely the idolatry due to Darius.

14 The king suddenly realized what had happened—that he had been a tool in the hands of his two presidents and the satraps. (i) He was "sore displeased *with himself.*" This appears to be the only case in the Scriptures where there is displeasure with self. Here it was mere natural displeasure, but spiritually speaking this can be the first stage in recognition of sin and hence of the need for repentance and salvation. (ii) Daniel must have been a favourite president of the king, so he tried to "deliver him" no doubt by using lawyers backed by all the laws of the Medes and the Persians. But there could be no loophole possible in this legally enacted decree to prevent its execution. Darius could not have the ultimate say in the matter, unlike Nebuchadnezzar who, as an absolute dictator, could have done what he liked!

15 The conspirators sensed a delay, so they reminded the king of the general principles of their law—nothing could be changed. It may seem surprising that even some believers cannot or will not perceive the unalterable principles for life and service in the Word of God. Modern conditions are allowed to bring in modern practices, the Word of God being treated as too old-fashioned in some respects to abide by it.

Deliverance from the Den of Lions, 6.16-28

16   Naturally, the king had lost his cause, but spiritually , by saying "Thy God whom thou servest continually, he will deliver thee," his "faith" was formed by the stedfast faith and practice of Daniel. He said, "*Thy* God," not because He was unique for Darius, for he still believed in his gods and that he was their representation, but because the king knew that Daniel had but one God. Moreover, Daniel served his God "continually." Darius knew the habits of his chief president! Thus in Acts 2.42 the church in Jerusalem "continued stedfastly"; in Acts 6.4 the apostles gave themselves "continually" to prayer and the ministry of the Word; in Luke 24.53, they were "continually" in the temple praising and blessing God. In spite of any dangers around, nothing can deflect a stedfast faithful man.

Moreover, Darius knew that God would "deliver" Daniel. This is remarkable, since the king had only known Daniel for a short time! Of course this knowledge did not justify Darius putting God to the test by casting Daniel into the den of lions. Darius stands in contrast to Nebuchadnezzar, Dan. 3.15, who in rage and fury had had the three men cast into the furnace *with no thought of God at all.*

17   The stone and the seal were almost a type of the Lord's burial, Matt. 27.60-66. In Daniel's case, it was to keep him in, with no possibility of rescue as *alive*. In the Lord's case, it was to keep His body safe in *death*, since the priests and Pharisees thought that the disciples would remove it. The disciples had no anticipation of the Lord's resurrection.

Many seals were used on this stone at the entrance to the den. The seals of the lords were used, since they must have distrusted the king; had his seal only been used, it could have been secretly broken to attempt to secure Daniel's release, and then resealed. But God works behind the seals and locks of men.

18   The king had a guilty conscience all night; he had been responsible for the situation through his own lack of care. No natural means such as fasting, and no artificial means such as music could give him relief. Music of the harp had been able to give king Saul relief centuries before, but the conviction of sin cannot be dismissed by such means. As in the case of the second Saul, "it is hard for thee to kick against the pricks," Acts 9.5. So the king had no sleep that night—quite a different night from that passed a short time before by Belshazzar whose idolatrous feasting led to his death, Dan. 5.1,30.

19   In great anxiety, Darius went to the den early in the morning (reminding us of the early visit to the Lord's tomb while it was still dark, John 20.1). The previous kings would not have bothered to go, believing that nothing could save prisoners' lives, since this was a common means of execution.

20 By crying "O Daniel, servant of the living God," the king clearly exhibited a touch of faith in Daniel's God. In verse 16, by saying "he will deliver thee," he expressed certainty, but now in verse 20 he merely asked a question, "is thy God . . . able to deliver thee?" When compared with monarchs such as Pharaoh, Sennacherib, Herod or Nero, he was an exception. Note the reason why he thought that God could intervene; it was because of Daniel's testimony, "whom thou servest continually."

21 Daniel was alive! He used a polite form of address, recognizing the king's authority, "O king, live for ever," knowing that the king would not live for ever. He knew the onward march of the kings and the kingdoms.

22 The prophet's explanation lay in "My God"—not Darius' gods. Such a personal relationship is precious to all God's people. Both Thomas and Paul used this personal title, John 20.28; Phil. 4.19, while the Lord used this holy title when suffering on the cross, Psa. 22.1; Matt. 27.46. It was Daniel's God who had sent "his angel," though who this was is not defined. Previously, Nebuchadnezzar had used the word "angel" for one whom he called "the Son of God," Dan. 3.25.28. The angel whom God had sent to the den of lions may have been an O.T. theophany, though God often used angels as such to be agents of His power, as in Herod's case, Acts 12.23, (the word "angel" meaning messenger).

This angel "shut the lions' mouths"—this was direct physical protection from their teeth and also from their paws. The writer to the Hebrews interpreted this event as "the prophets: who through faith . . . stopped the mouths of lions," Heb. 11.33. Paul likewise could testify that "I was delivered out of the mouth of the lion," 2 Tim. 4.17, that is, the Lord stood with him to deliver him from the emperor Nero, but at the end of his life the apostle had to suffer martyrdom. Both Daniel and Paul were such that "innocency was found" in them before God, and Daniel had "done no hurt" to the king. For 70 years Daniel had had this testimony; there was never any practical blame attached to him by God; there was never any deliberate breaking of the laws of God. Centuries before, David had been surrounded by evil doers, but personally he said "I will wash my hands in innocency: so will I compass thine altar, O Lord," Psa. 26.5,6, the whole Psalm showing how innocency attached to him.

23 Darius now exerted his authority; Daniel was released. How often we find this happy occasion in Scripture. Thus they brought Joseph "hastily out of the dungeon," Gen. 41.14; after 37 years captivity, the king of Babylon "did lift up the head of Jehoiachin king of

Judah out of prison," 2 Kings 25.27; "they drew up Jeremiah with cords, and took him out of the dungeon," Jer. 38.13; there were the experiences of Peter, Acts 5.19; 12.7-11, and that of Paul, 16.25-39. How all this is in keeping with the words of Isaiah 61.1, "the opening of the prison to them that are bound." However, sometimes it was not God's will that there should be deliverance, as in the case of John the Baptist who was beheaded in prison, Matt. 14.10.

"No manner of hurt" was found in Daniel, similar to Daniel 3.27 where "the fire had no power." And the reason was "because he believed in his God," this being why Daniel appears (unnamed) in Hebrews 11.33. Faith overcame in a crisis, even in old age. Compare Paul's words in the storm, "I believe God, that it shall be even as it was told me," Acts 27.25.

24   The conspirators then met a similar end without deliverance. All the men of verse 7 were included, and so the kingdom needed a whole new set of administrators apart from Daniel. The lions' mouths were not stopped on this second occasion; there was immediate judgment of a terrible kind. "Be sure your sin will find you out," Num. 32.23. It may appear to have been a cruel custom to cast the wives and children into the den as well. But contrast this with the case of Korah, when "the earth opened her mouth, and swallowed them up, and their houses, and all the men that appertained unto Korah, and all their goods," Num. 16.32. Yet later we read, "the children of Korah died not," 26.11, evidently so that their subsequent generations could take part in the O.T. service of tabernacle and temple. In a sense, these acts of judgment are pre-pictures of the final judgment in the lake of fire, Rev. 20.15.

25   Darius then made a second decree based on better experience and principles. It was addressed to "all people, nations, and languages," the totality of nations forming the second kingdom. This was like the herald in Daniel 3.4, and Nebuchadnezzar in 3.29; 4.1. Darius' decree was almost like world-wide evangelism from the leader! This is unlike rulers today, for evangelists are often the lowliest of subjects, yet the most powerful in God's hands.

The "peace" issued by Darius was as in Daniel 4.1: it was formal but hardly spiritual. Only the Lord and His people can give expression to spiritual peace, so unlike the peace of the world's giving, John 14.27. In fact, true spiritual testimony is not propagated by a decree!

26   Certainly Darius spoke up for the living God and His kingdom. He deduced this from (i) Daniel as a stedfast faithful servant, and (ii) the miraculous deliverance. All men had to fear before the God of Daniel, though there was no command to put away their idolatrous gods. Darius could not have known the details of prophecy that so separated his kingdom from the eternal kingdom of the Son of man. He

may have thought that his own kingdom was also God's kingdom for ever.

27 By saying "He delivereth and rescueth," Darius appears to be thinking beyond the immediate deliverance of Daniel from the lions' den. There were the "signs and wonders in heaven and in earth." Did the king know anything of O.T. history where the signs and wonders were displayed before the Jewish nation? Signs suggest divine intervention with object lessons within them; wonders suggest that the interventions show the divine Person working them out. In Acts 2.22, signs and wonders are associated with the Lord Jesus; in Hebrews 2.4 with the apostles, but in 2 Thessalonians 2.9 and Revelation 13.12-15 they are associated with the anti-Christ, the man of sin and the false prophet—yes, with Satan himself. May we therefore discern carefully when confronted with events that are claimed to be signs and wonders!

28 Daniel had just a few more years left for his ministry—"in the reign of Darius, and in the reign of Cyrus." His exercise before God in chapter 9 would be fulfilled, and there would be the liberation of some of the captivity sor the rebuilding of the temple in Jerusalem in the first year of Cyrus, Ezra 1.1-4.

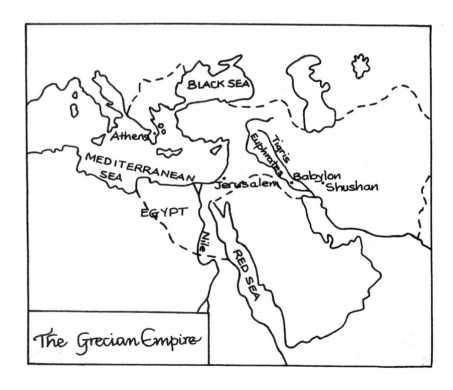

The Grecian Empire

Part 3

DANIEL THE PROPHET

Chapter 7
The Panorama of the Four Beasts

Thus far in the Book, chapters 1-6 have been historical, stretching chronologically from the beginning of the Babylonian kingdom to the beginning of the Medo-Persian kingdom; Daniel developed from a young man into old age throughout this period. Interspersed are Nebuchadnezzar's two dreams and Daniel's interpretation of them. Chapters 7-12 are again chronological, though embracing a much shorter period, stretching from just **before** the end of the first kingdom to just **after** the beginning of the second. In his old age, Daniel now has visions concerning the times of the Gentiles, Luke 21.24.

Chapter 7 refers to the **first** year of Belshazzar—four beasts represent the four major kingdoms, leading up to Messiah's kingdom. Chapter 8 refers to the **third** year of Belshazzar — two further beasts represent the second and third kingdoms, leading up to a historical type of enmity against God's people in the last times. Chapter 9 refers to the first year of Darius, with Daniel in prayer anticipating the end of the 70 years captivity; he was granted information about the 70 weeks of prophecy, leading up to the last week yet to come. Chapters 10-12 form a connected vision that was granted in the **third** year of Cyrus. This leads historically up to Antiochus Epiphanes, and then prophetically to the anti-Christ, to the future king of the north, and to events concerning the Jewish nation in the last times.

Chapter 2 concerns the vision of the kingdoms as Nebuchadnezzar viewed both them and himself—his wishful thinking of the gold-kingdom. Chapter 7 is concerned with **God's viewpoint** of kingdoms and dictators—they are seen as beasts. As Joseph said of Pharaoh's two dreams, "The dream of Pharaoh is one," Gen. 41.25, so we believe that chapters 2 and 7 of Daniel refer to the same four kingdoms from entirely different points of view. We recognize that there is a minority of expositors who state that the four beasts in Daniel 7 all refer to the ultimate future, but their arguments in support of this hypothesis seem weak and flat; we cannot support this idea, and hence take the view of the majority of expositors that the two chapters refer to the same four kingdoms, terminating with the kingdom of the Stone and the Son of man.

Verses 1-8 present four beasts, a beast being a common concept in the Bible. "Man that is in honour, and understandeth not, is like the beasts that perish," Psa. 49.20, showing that ignorance of divine things reduces men to that level. And then men seek to reduce God to that level as well, "they . . . changed the glory of the uncorruptible God into an image made like to corruptible man, and to birds, and fourfooted beasts," Rom. 1.23.

Verses 9-14 show activity in heaven leading to the destruction of the fourth and last kingdom, and the introduction of the kingdom of the Son of man.

Verses 15-28 describe the fourth beast in greater detail.

The Four Beasts Rising from the Sea, 7.1-8

1   The first year of Belshazzar occurred well over sixty years after the events described in chapter 1. Daniel was about 80 years old, a man of mature faithfulness, experience and spiritual learning. Only then could he have had such important visions to record for posterity. In fact, this is the first recorded vision that Daniel had. Note that he "wrote" the dream, as well as "told" it. Whether what he wrote is what we have in the O.T., or whether it was some other document, we are not informed. Certainly all the major prophets engaged in writing. Thus Isaiah had to take a great roll and write, Isa. 8.1; Baruch wrote at the dictation of Jeremiah, Jer. 36.4,32; 45.1; whereas Ezekiel was given a roll "written within and without," Ezek. 2.9,10, yet he himself had to write all the laws of the restored house, 43.11. It is what is written that constitutes "a more sure word of prophecy" rather than what is seen, however vivid the memory of events, 2 Pet. 1.19. John also had to "write the things" which he had seen, Rev. 1.19.

2   The fact that Daniel had a "vision" shows that his declaration was not his own ideas, his own understanding of the O.T. Scriptures, or his own reinterpretation of the dream-image of chapter 2. Rather, the vision originated from God.

The "four winds" speak of universal upheavals amongst nations and men (quite the opposite to the "sound from heaven as of a rushing mighty wind," Acts 2.2). These were Satanic forces, bringing conflict among nations and their leaders, thereby deposing nations and establishing militarily superior nations and kingdoms. God used these means to ensure that His will would be done at all stages in the onward progress of the times of the Gentiles. Only partially can the "great sea" be understood as the Mediterranean Sea, in the surrounds of which these great events would take place. Rather these beasts arose from the turbulence and volatility of the multitude of peoples; "Woe to the multitude of many people, which make a noise like the noise of the seas; and to the rushing of nations, that make a rushing like the rushing of mighty waters," Isa. 17.12; "the waters . . . are peoples, and multitudes, and nations, and tongues," Rev. 17.15. People are manipulated by their leaders and by Satan, for the last beast additionally rises out of the bottomless pit, Rev. 17.8.

3   These four great beasts are the four kingdoms of men that span the times of the Gentiles. They correspond to the four metals in order from top to bottom in Daniel 2.31-43. A "beast" denotes God's estimate of political and national power and what it seeks to achieve. In Daniel 8.4 the plural word "beasts" shows that all nations are described under this title. In Revelation 13.1, the beast out of the sea represents the dictator and kingdom of the last times after the rapture of the church (the second beast in verse 11 denotes the anti-Christ, the false prophet, the man of sin). (The reader should not confuse these beasts with the four "beasts" around the throne, Rev. 4.6-9, for this is a different Greek word meaning "living creatures.") The political beast of verse 1 is like "a leopard, a bear, a lion," v.2, having in the end times the character of the three beasts that precede it in Daniel 7. 4-6. The fourth beast in Daniel 7.7 must, in the last times, be equated to the beast in Revelation 13.1; both are nameless.

All the four beasts are "diverse one from another"—they would all have different characteristics, policies, cruelty, and attitudes to God and to His people and their service. Originally at Babel, God determined the bounds of the habitation of the nations, Gen. 11.8; Acts 17.26, but thereafter due to power-hungry dictators it has been fashionable to absorb and to merge. Thus Nebuchadnezzar and his successors brought together many nations by their conquests.

4   **Kingdom I: the Babylonian kingdom** lasting for 66 years. This is consistently denoted by "a lion." "The lion is come up from his thicket, and the destroyer of the Gentiles is on his way," Jer. 4.7; "a lion out of the forest shall slay them . . . because their transgressions are many," 5.6; "Israel is a scattered sheep; the lions have driven him away . . . and last this Nebuchadnezzar king of Babylon hath broken the

bones," 50.17. The "wings" denote the width and ease of conquest, the power and might of Nebuchadnezzar: "he shall fly as an eagle, and shall spread his wings over Moab," 48.40; "he shall come up and fly as the eagle," 49.22; "a great eagle with great wings . . . Know ye not what these things mean? . . . the king of Babylon is come to Jerusalem," Ezek. 17.3,12. Thus Nebuchadnezzar took Chaldea, Assyria, Arabia, Syria, Egypt, Palestine, but suddenly stopped his conquests; no doubt cessation occurred when he was reformed by God in Daniel 4, for he ultimately had a "man's heart." In 4.16 his heart was changed to that of a beast for seven years, but his understanding later returned and he issued "peace" to all nations, vs. 1,34.

    5 **Kingdom II: the Medo-Persian kingdom** lasting for just over 200 years. This is the silver kingdom of Daniel 2.32,39, described as "inferior." As a bear, it was seen "on one side," or "of one dominion," denoting the union of the Medes and the Persians, the union of the silver breast and arms, the existence of the two horns of the ram, one higher than the other, 8.3. It would "devour much flesh," its character being massive, cruel, ferocious, bloodthirsty and insatiable. Seen from today's vantage point, the "three ribs in the mouth of it" would be the nations of Libya, Egypt and Babylon. As the ram in 8.4, its aggressive ambitions would cause it to push westwards, northwards and southwards; no nations could stand before its thrusts, and the leadership of this second kingdom would do "according to his will."

    6 **Kingdom III: the Grecian kingdom** lasting for just over 300 years. It was represented by the lower parts of the body of the image made of brass, Dan. 2.32. Although this kingdom is named as that of Greece in 8.21, the fulfilment of this prophecy took place in the intertestamental period, after the O.T. closed and before the N.T. opened. Apart from prophetic details in Scripture, its history must be traced in the pages of profane history. (Prophetically, its details are traced in Daniel 8.8-25; 11.3-32, the objective being to trace history up to the Syrian king Antiochus Epiphanes as a type of the enmity against God's people that is yet to come.) The military government of Greece had as its first king Alexander the Great, who defeated the millions of men in the Medo-Persian army with but a relatively small army sweeping over the land even to northern India.

    In Daniel 7.6, the symbol of a leopard is suitable to depict art, culture and civilization. "Can a leopard change its spots?" asked the Lord through Jeremiah, Jer. 12.23, and truly Greek culture has lasted over the centuries even though the empire has long since passed away, as witnessed by school children for decades having to learn Pythagoras' theorem in geometry. Moreover, the leopard had "four wings," speaking of rapid conquest in all directions, all achieved while Alexander was a young man. He died in Babylon at the early age of 33; since there was no heir, the conquered territory was divided into four parts under the leadership of four generals. These were the "four heads," Egypt (south of Jerusalem) and Syria (north and north-east of Jerusalem) being two of the parts.

In Daniel 8.5, this kingdom is described as "an he goat" from the west (from Greece), having "a notable horn." This is defined in verse 21 as being "the first king," namely Alexander the Great. In verse 8, this great horn is broken, being replaced by "four notable ones," namely the four generals, who headed "four kingdoms," v.22. In 11.4, Alexander's kingdom is again seen as "broken," and "divided toward the four winds of heaven," again referring to the four parts ruled over by the four generals. The object of both chapter 8 and 11 is to trace the history of one part, namely Syria, and the rise of its king Antiochus Epiphanes as a historical type of future enmity against God's people in a sense to be described in chapter 8.

7 Kingdom IV: the Roman kingdom following Greece, seen as lasting up to the time of the establishment of Messiah's kingdom. This fourth beast has no name given to it (neither in Revelation 13.1). No real animal on earth could adequately describe pictorially the status of this kingdom. Its brutality and its conquest distinguish it from all others. Although Rome is not mentioned by name in O.T. prophecy, this fourth kingdom must be Rome (appearing so often in the N.T.), for it followed the Grecian kingdom which gradually collapsed over the century preceding the birth of the Lord Jesus. And no other kingdom of men is foreseen in either chapter 2 or chapter 7. Messiah's kingdom will follow: the God of heaven shall set up a kingdom, to be ruled over by the Stone, 2.44,45; the last beast shall be slain, to be replaced by the Son of man, 7.11-13. It was Rome that crucified the Lord Jesus, that destroyed Jerusalem in A.D. 70, that slaughtered millions of Jews, that persecuted Christians, causing many to be put to death. The Roman emperors ruled over all, and ultimately Rome polluted the church by leading to papal Rome. It was essentially the Roman kingdom that Satan offered to the Lord Jesus during the time of His temptation, Matt. 4.8-10.

This beast "stamped the residue" with its feet; no doubt this refers to the Jews, who have been, and who will be so evilly treated by this nation. And suddenly at the end of verse 7, by the words "and it had ten horns," the prophecy turns to the distant future. Corresponding to the ten toes of the image, we have here the final development of the fourth kingdom, the amalgamation of many nations, though rather distinct from the ten horns and ten kings of Revelation 17.12.

8 As we have said, to fit in with the overall view of prophetic history, verse 8 must refer to the end times. The "gap" of the church age, which is not the subject of prophecy, must be inserted towards the end of verse 7, though this would not be known to readers in O.T. times. The fact that the fourth kingdom is divided into two periods is confirmed by Revelation 17.8, where the beast "was, and is not, and yet is"; the verb "was" refers to past imperial Rome; the verb "is not" refers to the church age, and the verb "yet is" refers to the future. This distinction is **not** apparent in the O.T.

Daniel saw "another little horn," the future dictator of the revived Roman empire—the word "little" means that it will have an insignificant beginning. It will have a "mouth speaking great things"; it will "speak great words against the most High," v.25; it will prevail against the saints, wearing them out for three and a half years, vs. 21,25. (Note that this "little horn" is the political leader, corresponding to the **first** beast in Revelation 13. The "little horn" in Daniel 8.9 refers to Antiochus Epiphanes, a type of enmity against God's people. This enmity is yet to appear, and corresponds on the one hand to the anti-Christ as the **second** beast in Revelation 13, and on the other hand to the king of the north; this will be explained in the next chapter.) In this future time, instability will mark the political scene until the beast gains complete control. Thus in our verse three kings are deposed, leaving seven.

In Revelation 17.3, there are seven heads and ten horns. The seven heads may refer to those remaining in Daniel 7.9; five seem to fall, Rev. 17.10. The "ten horns" refer to a second grouping of ten kings, who aid the beast in his adventurism at the battle of Armageddon, when all of them will turn their weapons against the descending Lamb, v.14. There seems to be complete political confusion, with the beast toppling authorities that he cannot agree with. In Daniel 7, the prophetic eye saw the symbolism enacted, but a full interpretation is not given.

Activity in Heaven, and the Kingdom of the Son of Man, 7.9-14

9 We now come up to the time to which so much of the Bible looks. It culminates in the Book of Revelation, and was so often anticipated by the Lord in the Gospels. We have the judgment of the nations and all their political systems, man having failed in his responsibility given him during the times of the Gentiles, as the Jews had failed before. The Lord had said that His kingdom "is not of the world," John 18.36, but men will continue to grasp authority until all power and authority is confined to the hands of the Son of man. There will be no lasting peace on earth until this coming great event.

The thrones being "cast down" means that they were "set." It does not refer to the thrones of the beast and his subsidiary kings being destroyed, v.11. Rather it refers to thrones situated around the central throne occupied by the One who is "Holy, holy, holy," Rev. 4.2. (For example, there are twenty-four "seats"—meaning "thrones"—around the central throne, v.4.) Additionally, the Lord said to His apostles, "ye also shall sit upon twelve thrones," Matt. 19.28; "that ye may . . . sit on thrones judging the twelve tribes of Israel," Luke 22.29,30. Again, we read John's testimony, "I saw thrones, and they sat upon them . . . and they lived and reigned with Christ a thousand years," Rev. 20.4. These thrones were thus being prepared.

The dominant One in Daniel's vision was "the Ancient of days," also described as the "Lord God Almighty, which was, and is, and is to come," Rev. 4.8, (note how the verb "and is" contrasts with "and is not" applied to the beast, 17.8). This Name refers to God's eternal character in the **past**, while the idea behind "an everlasting dominion," Dan. 7.14, shows His eternal character in the **future**. His garment being as white as snow refers to His infinite righteousness in judgment, for "he shall judge the world with righteousness," Psa. 96.13, and "righteousness and judgment are the habitation of his throne," 97.2. His hair being like pure wool shows the reverence due to this Eternal One who judges righteously; see Rev. 1.14. This throne radiated fire—fire that removes the dross in our service, 1 Cor. 3.13-15, and fire that judges others, 2 Thess. 1.8. Thus Nadab, Abihu and Korah were judged by this means, Lev. 10.2; Num. 16.35. In fact, the throne is visualized here like a chariot with burning wheels, "the Lord will come with fire, and with his chariots like a whirlwind," Isa. 66.15.

10   Daniel saw the throne prepared for fiery judgment, from which there could be no relief when it fell upon "them that know not God, and that obey not the gospel of our Lord Jesus Christ," 2 Thess. 1.8. Other descriptions of this time are: "thy wrath is come," Rev. 11.18; "Thrust in thy sharp sickle," 14.18; "a sharp sword, that with it he should smite the nations," 19.15; "Gather ye together first the tares, and bind them in bundles to burn them," Matt. 13.30.

In Revelation 5, the throne was set for judgments on earth during the last seven years of Gentile domination, but our verse 10 describes the judgment court of heaven in readiness for the coming of the Lord in glory. Certainly the scene is in heaven prior to a final judgment effected on earth. The scene demonstrates the capacity and righteousness of the throne about to be active in judgment. Who the "thousand thousands . . . and ten thousand times ten thousand" might be was apparently unknown to Daniel, but the scene answers to Revelation 5.11 where this number of angels surround the throne in praise, and to 7.9 where there is a great multitude "which no man could number" from the nations who had come out of the great tribulation.

In Revelation 6, there were broken the seals of the book of the counsels of God with the recipe for righteous judgment committed to the Lamb.

"The books were opened" in our verse are distinct from this, and appear to be the deeds of men about to be judged on earth just **prior** to the establishment of Messiah's millennial kingdom. Clearly the scene is different from that in Revelation 20.12, where "the books were opened . . . and the dead were judged out of those things which were written in the books, according to their works," for this takes place **after** the millennial reign —in fact 1,000 years later at the great white throne judgment.

11 Both the horn and the fourth beast are mentioned here. In Daniel 7.17,23, the beast is both the king and the kingdom. Which is implied the context must determine. We suggest that the beast represents both the first king of this empire, and the developed kingdom thereafter. The horns were subsidiary kings, while the little horn is the final king. In Revelation 13-19, the beast stands for the leader of the last kingdom, able to speak blasphemies for forty-two months, 13.5,6. And it is this leader, together with the anti-Christ, who will be judged without passing through ordinary physical death, 19.20. The rest were slain to await the judgment of the great white throne. So in our verse 11, the destruction of the king and his empire is visualized. "For he shall have judgment without mercy, that hath showed no mercy," James 2.13.

12 Daniel would wonder what was going to happen to the previous three beasts. This vision was taking place towards the end of the first kingdom, so none of the beasts had so far passed away in Daniel's experience. The ends of the kingdoms of the lion, bear and leopard were not at all obvious. Consequently, in verse 12 the statement is made that the other three beasts "had their dominion taken away," implying that their ends would come in keeping with the divine will. In other words, these kingdoms could no longer exert any power and authority, since more powerful rulers took over. Yet "their lives were prolonged for a season and a time"—for rather an indefinite period. In fact, when the various take-overs of power took place, the peoples remained, the population grew, along with their customs and culture. Thus Babylon continued as Babylon when Cyrus and Darius took the kingdom. In fact, Persia and Greece still exist as local nations today, but with none of the power of former years. We have already noted that the dictator in Revelation 13.2 will use all that he needs of the leopard, bear and lion kingdoms.

13 We now have Christ's kingdom established when Gentile rule has been swept away. In verses 8 and 9, many features from the Book of Revelation are to be seen. Here we have more. Thus the "Son of man," featured in Ezekiel and Daniel, as well as in Psalm 80.17, is the title of the Lord Jesus in Manhood power (in His life here on earth; in future judgment and in future display); it is the title by which the Lord always referred to Himself. Coming with "the clouds of heaven" is found many times in the N.T. As far as the Church is concerned, we shall meet

the Lord in the clouds at His descent, 1 Thess. 4.16,17. As far as concerns the time of which Daniel 7.13 speaks, the Lord said, "they shall see the Son of man coming in the clouds of heaven with power and great glory," Matt. 24.30; "he cometh with clouds; and every eye shall see him," Rev. 1.7; 14.14. No doubt these clouds are more than physical clouds—He will come with "so great a cloud of witnesses," men of faith throughout the ages, Heb. 12.1.

"They brought him near before him" seems to answer to Revelation 5.6,7, where the Lamb as it had been slain came to the One seated on the throne to take the book. It is the triumph of the Lamb before the throne prior to His open triumph and display on earth.

    14   As brought to the throne, He was given "dominion, and glory, and a kingdom." We feel that this took place **before** the judgment of the beast in verse 11. It corresponds to the praise recorded in Revelation 5.9-14, "Worthy is the Lamb . . . to receive power." Men brought Him in honour and esteem to Jerusalem, riding upon an ass. Here, He is brought to an investiture in heaven: "Yet have I set my king upon my holy hill of Zion . . . Ask of me, and I shall give thee the heathen for thine inheritance," Psa. 2.6-8.

The result was that, when the Stone filled the whole earth, "all people, nations, and languages, should serve him." These are Jews and Gentiles who enter the kingdom, the "sheep" who inherit the kingdom, Matt. 25.33-40, "the nations of them which are saved . . . and the kings of the earth" who bring their glory and honour, Rev. 21.24. How unlike any Gentile kingdom described in Daniel or that has existed in subsequent history! Moreover, this kingdom is "everlasting" and one "which shall not be destroyed." This answers to Gabriel's promise to Mary, "he shall reign . . . for ever; and of his kingdom there shall be no end," Luke 1.23. The 1,000 years on earth will be followed by the delivering up of the kingdom to God for eternity, 1 Cor. 15.24.

The Fourth Beast Interpreted, 7.15-28

    15   Daniel was greatly troubled since he did not know the meaning, particularly of the fourth beast. In earlier chapters, under the hand of God he had been able to interpret dreams other than his own. But his own dreams needed direct heavenly interpretation to his mind. See also Daniel 8.27; 10.8, where the prophet was likewise in trouble of mind and body.

    16   We are not told who "one of them that stood by" really was. No doubt an angel, but later it was Gabriel, 8.16. Daniel could not invent his own interpretation, for "no prophecy . . . is of any private interpretation," 2 Pet. 1.20. So Daniel asked, and then he received, in keeping with the Lord's words, "Ask, and it shall be given you," Matt.

7.7. John too had many things explained to him in his vision on Patmos, Rev. 7.14; 17.7.

17 Daniel is told that the four beasts are "four *kings*, which shall arise out of the earth." This fact has not appeared before in the chapter so far, though in our exposition we have used this fact, but for Daniel the interpretation had not been mingled with the dream itself. "Beasts" is how God sees the actual character of Gentile rule, unlike the glory of the image in chapter 2 which shows this character from man's point of view. In 7.3, these beasts came from the "sea," namely arising from the totality of peoples and nations. But here, they arise from the "earth." This evidently is presented as a contrast to heaven, v.13; "Ye are from beneath; I am from above," John 8.23. (In Revelation 13.11, the religious beast—the false prophet and the anti-Christ—arises "out of the earth," but there it must be interpreted as the Jewish homeland.)

The word "shall" in our verse presents no difficulty. It might be said that the first king and empire had already arisen over 60 years previously, and that the future tense can only be applied to the remaining three kings and empires. But Daniel's vantage point in the vision must be taken as in the past, just prior to the beginning of the times of the Gentiles. (This is similar to the prophecy in Revelation 12, where John's vantage point was many years previously prior to the birth of the Lord, Jesus.)

18 The angel immediately goes to the distant future, to what is pleasing rather than to what is displeasing. "The saints of the most High shall take the kingdom"—in a greater measure than when Darius took the kingdom, 5.31. The "most High" refers either to God or to the heavenly places; we shall refer to this again when we discuss verse 25. This latter verse shows that "the saints" refer to God's people on earth during the great tribulation. Seen from our knowledge of the N.T. Scriptures, we recognize that the N.T. saints will also be included in this kingdom. We are saints of the heavenly places, Eph. 1.3, and as overcomers in the Church age we will eventually reign with Christ over the nations, Rev. 2.26,27; 3.21. How true it is that we can see Christ in a verse such as our verse 18, for "the testimony of Jesus is the spirit of prophecy," Rev. 19.10, that is, the object of the inspiring Spirit of God is to testify of the glories of Christ.

This kingdom lasts "for ever, even for ever and ever," in sharp contrast to all the kingdoms of the beasts. We may quote a verse of the hymn "The day Thou gavest, Lord, is ended":

> So be it, Lord, Thy throne shall never,
> Like earth's proud empires, pass away;
> Thy kingdom stands, and grows for ever,
> Till all Thy creatures own Thy sway.

19 Daniel was not completely satisfied with this brief explanation;
      he wanted to know further details—"the truth about the fourth
beast." So this subject occupies the rest of the chapter. By the "truth,"
there is meant an interpretation from heaven and not from men, for
Daniel was wise to all the methods of men, and would completely avoid
them where the things of God were concerned. Verse 19 repeats verse 7.
The power in the teeth, claws and feet is what an animal uses in the
destruction of its prey. The "iron" corresponds to the cruel methods
peculiar to itself as the iron kingdom, 2.40; the "brass" copies what was
useful from the third kingdom, 2.39, as indicated in Revelation 13.2. We
feel that "the residue" answers to the people of God, whether devout
Jews or sincere Christians according to the dispensation in which the
beast as Rome is operating.

20 This repeats verse 8. It speaks of the rise of this particular leader
      in addition to the ten kings of which three would fall. This is not
speculation in past history, but relates to a future confederation of
smaller kingdoms over which the beast will assume control. He is
described as "stout," a common Hebrew word in the O.T., translated
once by "stout," "many" 190 times and "great" 128 times. Thus the word
describes the pre-eminence of this beast over his contemporary leaders,
and hence seems to be a copy of the pre-eminence of the Lord Himself.

21 We now have new information, not given previously in the
      chapter. The "war with the saints" constitutes the great tribula-
tion, Dan. 12.1, when there will be political, religious and military subjugation of God's people by this dictator, by the anti-Christ, and by the
king of the north. (Before his conversion, Saul made war with the
saints—even with the Lord Himself—but this verse does not refer to
that.) Rather, this warfare will be unique, "there shall be a time of trouble, such as never was since there was a nation even to that same time,"
12.1; "great tribulation, such as was not since the beginning of the world
to this time, no, nor ever shall be," Matt. 24.21; "the beast . . . shall
make war against them (the two witnesses)," Rev. 11.7; "it was given unto him to make war with the saints, and to overcome them," 13.7. It
looks as if the beast would gain the victory, by seeking to stamp out the
things of God altogether, but the time will be shortened.

22 The only way to deal with the mushroom growth of the
      kingdom of the beast is through the direct intervention of "the
Ancient of days," through the advent of the Son of man in glory. At that
time, "judgment was given to the saints." This does not mean that they
will actively participate in acts of judgment that are the right of Christ
alone; "He doth judge" and He shall "smite the nations," Rev. 19.11,15,
but the saints accompany Him upon white horses. Rather they will judge
during the kingdom rule of the Lord; "judgment was given unto them,"

Rev. 20.4. They will then possess the kingdom, in the sense of being its members, and ruling with Christ, 2.26,27.

23 Again the angelic interpreter returns to the subject of the fourth beast. The interpretation given in verse 17, where the beasts are stated to be four kings, is extended to include kingdoms. The fourth kingdom will be the worst, and different from all others. It will be more brutal, more motivated by tyranny, more expansive in its aspirations after territorial aggrandisement, breaking everything before it. "The whole earth" will be greater than the boundaries of Solomon's kingdom, that stretched "from the river (Euphrates) even unto the land of the Philistines, and to the border of Egypt," 2 Chron. 9.26.

24 The little horn is seen as rising from amongst a grouping of ten horns or kings. This confederation is yet future; Rome as an empire ceased in the fifth century, and the so-called "clock" of prophecy does not start again until after the rapture of the Church. Then the eleventh horn will subdue three, leaving seven besides himself. After that, five more fall, Rev. 17.10, but to have enough power to eliminate the religious apostate and harlot Babylon the great, he gains the support of ten more horns or kings, vs. 12,16.

25 The activity of this dictator will be (i) to utter "great words against the most High"; this had been the activity of the religious leaders when the Lord was here. "He opened his mouth in blasphemy against God . . . and his tabernacle, and them that dwell in heaven," Rev. 13.6; see 16.11. This reference to both God and His tabernacle allows us to interpret "the most High" as either the most High God, or the heavenly places. (ii) He will "wear out the saints," such as causing men to have the mark of the beast before they can buy or sell, 13.17. (iii) He will "change times and laws." Expositors understand "times" to refer to established customs and institutions built up over the years; dictators seek to eliminate what is cherished from the past, seeking to introduce their own ideas of utopia. "Laws" will be changed, no doubt working in conjunction with the anti-Christ; Jewish sabbaths and feasts will be vulnerable, as well as true testimony in Christ's Name. This will take place in the middle of the last week (that is, seven years), Dan. 9.27, when "the sacrifice and the oblation" will be made to cease. The duration of this change will be the period known as "a time and times and the dividing of time," or forty-two months.

26 However, the court of heaven will sit; the Ancient of days will pronounce, and the Son of man will execute the sentence . "They shall take away his dominion" will mark the end of Gentile rule. In Daniel 5.28-31, the second ruler and kingdom terminated the rule of the first beast, but here the Lord Himself terminates the rule of the last beast.

"To consume and to destroy it unto the end" may mean several things.

(i) The process of judgment takes place throughout the last seven years, until the final judgment in Revelation 19. In this process of burning and destruction, only the tares and the bad fish are eliminated, Matt. 13.30,41,42,48-50; the wheat and the good fish as the righteous shall "shine forth as the sun in the kingdom of their Father," v.43. (ii) Having been destroyed, the fourth kingdom remains destroyed up to the end of the 1,000 years reign of Christ. Then the nations are again gathered to battle, Rev. 20.7-10, but are destroyed never again to emerge in rebellion against God and His Christ.

27   The kingdom is now described—what a contrast to the previous verse. So the saints are triumphant after all!—as was the Lord, once crucified, but raised to glory. The persecuted saints are given the kingdom, which will be "everlasting" in contrast to the first four kingdoms of the beasts. Man on earth will be at last subject to the most High God, "when the people are gathered together, and the kingdoms, to serve the Lord," Psa. 102.22. The subjection of the saints will be such that they "obey him." This was necessary under the law, Exod. 19.5-8; it is necessary under the Gospel, Rom. 1.5; it will be necessary in the kingdom age.

28   The chapter concludes with the effect of all this on Daniel. In verse 15, he was grieved at the *vision*, but here he is troubled about the *interpretation*. The prophet could see the future trouble *for his own* people, and he was troubled on their behalf; see Luke 19.41-44. After all, this people were in enough trouble already, as captives in Babylon. Shortly, in chapter 9, before God Daniel would contemplate his people's release after 70 years captivity; similarly after the tribulation of the 70th week (the seven years after the rapture) there was going to be deliverance. History in Daniel's day was a picture of the future. In fact, as in the Lord's case, there was going to be glory after sufferings. Yet Daniel was saddened for a while, although there would be ultimate rejoicing. The disciples were sad at the thought of the Lord's death, but they would rejoice afterwards at His resurrection, John 16.20-22. "Weeping may endure for a night, but joy cometh in the morning," Psa. 30.5; 1 Pet. 1.6-11.

Chapter 8
Prophetic History of Enmity against God's People

Chapter 7 has led up to the fourth beast—the first beast of Revelation 13. In chapter 8 we now have a prophecy with a variety of objectives. To start with, most expositors agree that it leads up to the king of Syria known as Antiochus Epiphanes, whose character and activity allowed him to be presented as a prophetical type relating to the end times, this prophecy speaking of enmity against God's people in a sense to be developed later. Chapters 2-7 have dealt essentially with the nations, and are written in Aramaic; chapters 8-12 deal essentially with the Jews, and with Gentile opposition to them, so these chapters are written in Hebrew. Chapters 1-6 are written in the **third** person—the writer was writing about Daniel; but chapters 7-12 are written in the **first** person—Daniel writes about himself and his visions.

Several important personages strut around on the world stage in these future days.

(i) The emperor of the revived Roman empire, considered as the little horn in Daniel 7.8, as well as the first beast in Revelation 13. Since he will work hand-in-hand with the anti-Christ, we may call this **political** enmity against God's people.

(ii) The anti-Christ, the second beast in Revelation 13; we may term him the **religious** enemy against God's people.

(iii) The "king of the north," possessing this name in Daniel 11; he will be a future king of Syria and associated countries, and will be a **military** enemy of God's people. In Isaiah 10.5, he is called "O Assyrian, the rod of mine anger."

(iv) The "king of the south," possessing this name in Daniel 11, and having control over Egypt.

(v) "The chief prince" or "prince of Ros," Ezek. 38.2; 39.2 R.V., implying Russia, as can be strongly argued.

(vi) Mystery Babylon the great, Rev. 17,18, the worldwide corrupt system of religion into which Christendom will develop after the rapture.

The question is, which of the enemies of God's people are described in Daniel 8? It must be confessed that expositors differ in their understanding of the chapter. A few identify the "little horn" of 8.9 with the little horn of 7.8, namely with the leader of the revived Roman empire. We cannot subscribe to this view, since the origins, descriptions and activities of these two little horns are essentially different. Such expositors may or may not agree that the little horn in chapter 8 also refers to Antiochus Epiphanes.

Others assert that the little horn of chapter 8 is a type of the future anti-Christ, while yet others assert that he is a type of the future "king of the north." In other words, expositors see in the past activity of Antiochus Epiphanes features that will mark both the anti-Christ and the king of the north, but they ultimately opt for the one or for the other, arguing strongly for their contentions. It may therefore seem unwise to be too dogmatic. In fact, the structure of chapter 8 is quite unlike other chapters in Scripture that contain prophetic pronouncements. The immediate object of chapter 8 is to trace Medo-Persian, Grecian and Syrian history up to Antiochus Epiphanes, who is then used as a prophetic type of the future. Verses 2-14 describe the vision of the ram and the he-goat, **but** from verse 11 the description ceases to be symbolic and more directly that of a human personality. We believe that Antiochus is being described, but also a man of the future. In verses 15-26 the vision is interpreted by Gabriel; the two animals represent the second and third kingdoms, named in verses 20 and 21. Then the little horn, or Antiochus, is described, also implying a future personality. But **this description of the personality in the interpretation is quite unlike the description of the personality in the vision.** In fact, the description in the vision, vs. 10-12, stresses the activity of a **religious** enemy of God's people, while the description in verses 23-25 stresses the activity of a **military** enemy of God's people. Antiochus in past history engaged in both kinds of activity, but in the future, when things are worse, two different men will be prominent in these two directions.

So we feel that the Spirit of God in chapter 8 is laying bare the activities of both religious and military enemies against God's people in the end times. The present writer can therefore see more of the anti-Christ in verses 10-12, but more of the king of the north in verses 23-25. Both these personages come in chapter 11; verses 2-32 suggest history leading up to Antiochus, though they may also be indicative of events still future. Certainly after these verses the far future is described, with the king doing "according to his will" as the anti-Christ, v.36, together with "the king of the north" in verse 40, and to a lesser extent "the king of the south." So in our approach to chapter 8 we trace a helpful path that extracts useful suggestions from expositors who are more dogmatic in their production of seemingly conflicting explanations.

Daniel's Second Vision, 8.1-14

1   Two years after the vision of chapter 7, Daniel had his second vision; this suggests that visions came sparsely to Daniel in his

aged years. Belshazzar ruled for only three years, so the end of his kingdom was near when Daniel had this second vision. It is difficult to distinguish between visions and dreams, but a vision is more restricted to what a man is given to see (whether when asleep or in his waking hours). A dream is fuller, and refers to the hearing of words as well as seeing. This distinction is not unique, for in the vision in chapter 8 there are words at the end, v.13. Apart from that, this vision was one of sight only.

The forthcoming history of the second and third kingdoms is now going to be given in more detail (as the history of the fourth beast and kingdom had been given in detail in chapter 7). There was no need for the first kingdom to be described in detail, since Daniel had actually lived through it. "Where there is no vision, the people perish," Prov. 29.18: Daniel would live, but Belshazzar would perish.

2   Daniel's duties of state had taken him far and wide, and obviously he knew Shushan, in Persia over 200 miles east of Babylon. Our verse does not state that the vision took place there, but that he saw this place in a vision. Shushan was the capital of the Persian empire, so it is fitting that the events of the vision took place there. Nehemiah was there some 90 years later, Neh. 1.1, when he was exercised about the rebuilding of the wall of Jerusalem. The Book of Esther revolves around Shushan the palace where Ahasuerus had his throne, Esth. 1.2. The river Ulai was the name of a canal joining two rivers flowing past the city.

3   The vision needed Daniel to look up and not down, when he saw a ram with two horns. In 2.32, one had to look downwards from the head of gold in order to focus attention on the silver breast and arms—carrying the thought of duplication. In 7.5 the same empire as a bear was raised up on one side—two sides are implied, with one dominant above the other. Here, in our verse, this same ram-kingdom had two horns, though there was unequal duplication, "one was higher than the other." The ram stood symbolically for Persia: Persian kings wore a ram's head of gold, and their coins bore an image of a ram. So God used certain existing symbols for the substance of the vision. The higher horn stood for Cyrus, king of Persia, while the lower one stood for Darius the Mede.

4   This verse shows the development of the second kingdom, something that chapters 2 and 7 did not show. The Persians came from the east, pushing westwards (to Babylon, Syria), northwards (around the Caspian Sea), and southwards (to Egypt, Ethiopia and Palestine). None of the surrounding nations could be safe from its thrusts—note the word "beasts" in the plural, denoting these surroun-

ding nations, implying that not only the four great empires but also subsidiary nations were "beasts" in God's estimation. This expansion was only possible because the ram did "according to his will," namely man's will achieved God's plan for some nations to rise and others to fall. Was it not man's will that crucified the Lord Jesus in keeping with "the determinate counsel and foreknowledge of God"? Acts 2.23.

5   Two hundred years after Daniel, the he-goat of strength appeared on the scene, defined as "Grecia" in verse 21. The symbol of the goat was impressed upon the coins of Macedonia. The "notable horn" was the first king of Greece, v. 21, namely Alexander the Great. Note that this territory-seeking monarch came from the "west," whereas in verse 4 Cyrus came from the east. The verse describes Alexander's swift conquest in twelve years: he seemed to gain the world, including Egypt, Babylon, Persia and north-west India, his speed being graphically described as if he "touched not the ground."

6,7   The ram kingdom of Persia stood in his way, so he quickly defeated the huge armies of this second world empire amongst the Gentiles, and the brass-leopard kingdom was substituted. It may seem strange that such military adventurism should have succeeded; there were long lines of communication back to Greece, with distances over 1,400 miles involved. Yet strongholds were taken, Shushan was burnt, and the Medo-Persian army was completely overthrown. Ordinary history provides the details of Alexander's life and military conquests, but God allowed to happen exactly what had been prophesied in Daniel chapters 2,7,8.

8   At the height of his power, "very great" and "strong," this "great horn was broken." History tells us that, after a fever lasting eleven days, Alexander died at Babylon at the age of 33; he had been monarch of this rapidly growing empire for 13 years. He had no natural heir, so the kingdom was divided amongst four generals, "four notable ones toward the four winds of heaven," namely Greece, Asia Minor, Egypt (the province of the king of the south) and Babylon-Syria (the province of the king of the north).

9   The vision continues, but its parabolic substance gets less, and a certain amount of direct description of an actual personality breaks through. From one of the four quarters of this third empire, "a little horn" arose, quite different from the little horn of 7.8 which arose from the fourth kingdom. That in chapter 8 appears to be religious and military, while that in chapter 7 is political. As already explained, we believe that chapter 8 provides a historical type in a sense, both of the future anti-Christ and of the king of the north, whereas the little horn in chapter 7 was not typical, but a symbol of the real man yet to come. The little horn in chapter 8 "waxed exceeding great," pushing to the south (Egypt), to the east (Armenia), and to "the pleasant land," namely God's

land around Jerusalem. This is called a "pleasant land" in Jeremiah 3.19, and a "glorious land" in Daniel 11.16,41. In the history of the Grecian kingdom in the past, only one man answers to this description, and that is Antiochus Epiphanes—the "illustrious" one, who was king of Syria in the years B.C. 176-165. The description "little" corresponds to the fact that he was the younger son of a king of Syria; he had been in prison in Rome for many years, yet he ultimately seized power and sought expansion.

10   The sideways expansion in verse 9 was military; the upward expansion in verse 10 was religious. The "host of heaven" denotes God's people in Judaea at that time. (In other parts of the O.T., the "host of heaven" is a literal expression, denoting the direction of idolatrous worship, Deut. 4.19; Jer. 8.2.) The "stars" would refer to individual Jews who were persecuted, killed or cast down, as was the apostle Paul when he once described the attention that the enemies of the Gospel gave him, "we are made as the filth of the world, and are the offscouring of all things unto this day," 1 Cor. 4.13. Hebrews 11.34-38 describes some of the sufferings of that time; this affliction under Antiochus is also described in the books of the Maccabees, a non-inspired historical account found in the Apocrypha.

11   The pride of this man exalted itself even to "the prince of the host," a title which we understand refers to deity, in keeping with verse 25, "the Prince of princes." In the future, as in the past, "the kings of the earth (shall) set themselves . . . against the Lord," Psa. 2.2; he "exalteth himself above all that is called God . . . so that he as God sitteth in the temple of God, showing himself that he is God," 2 Thess. 2.4; as Satan exalted himself in time past by saying, "I will ascend into heaven, I will exalt my throne above the stars of God . . . I will be like the most High," Isa. 14.13,14.

In the vision, it was the temple of God that received the most direct attack. This Syrian king's activity outside in the court and inside the sanctuary was far worse than any desecration of altar and temple described in the Books of Kings and Chronicles. Antiochus plundered the temple for treasure; he forbad the keeping of the law, the observance of the burnt offering and sacrifice, the sabbaths and feast days; he polluted the sanctuary and those that were holy in its service. All this is typical of the activity of the anti-Christ of the future. Men today would often do this as regards the holy institutions of the Lord given in the N.T., and many pseudo-Christians flock to participate in this activity—the Corinthians treated the Lord's Supper in such a baseless manner, 1 Cor. 11.20,21.

12   The translation "an host was given him against the daily sacrifice by reason of transgression" is rather awkward to understand; a preferred translation is "a time of trial was appointed unto

the continual sacrifice by reason of transgression." Thus the "time of trial" caused by Antiochus was of limited duration, as allowed by God; see Matthew 24.22 where the trial of future days is shortened. The "transgression" totally was caused not only by the people and their evil ways, but by the high priest Jason who opened the temple gates so that Antiochus could enter. There were thus no powerful "porters" to guard "the gates of the house of the Lord, that none which was unclean in any thing should enter in," 2 Chron. 23.19. This recalls the local church visualized by Paul in Acts 20.29,30, where men from the **outside** and men from **within** would damage the spiritual status of the church at Ephesus.

The daily sacrifice could no longer be continued, and the horn "cast down the truth to the ground." Namely, all the holy ceremony of the law (truth, because originally given by God) was cast down, "for truth is fallen in the street, and equity cannot enter," Isa. 59.14. In the coming day, men will "believe a lie" because they will not receive "the love of the truth," 2 Thess. 2.10,11. When the Lord was here, He was "the truth," yet He was cast out and the leaders propagated lies about Him. The Lord knew that the pearls of truth, if cast before swine, would be trampled underfoot, Matt. 7.6, so He rejoiced that these things were hidden from the wise and prudent, 11.25.

Additionally, this little horn would practise and prosper. How often both then and today, can the righteous see the prosperity of the wicked. Thus Job asserted, "The tabernacles of robbers prosper, and they that provoke God are secure," Job 12.6; Asaph commented, "these are the ungodly, who prosper in the world; they increase in riches," Psa. 73.12; "I was envious at the foolish, when I saw the prosperity of the wicked," v.3; Jeremiah complained to God, "Wherefore doth the way of the wicked prosper?", Jer. 12.1; later he confessed as he gazed on the destruction of Jerusalem, "her enemies prosper," Lam. 1.5. God allows this for a little time, but not for ever.

13   Daniel may well have wondered how long this desecration of the service of God would last. But the question was asked for him, by "one saint" or "a holy one," no doubt an angel. This angel could also see what was going to happen, so asked how long these circumstances would last, as he spoke about the abolishing of the daily sacrifice and the sin that brought these desolations about. He was speaking of the temple in Jerusalem and "the host," God's faithful people amidst such darkness and apostasy.

How long? This question was asked dozens of times on the pages of Scripture, by hearts burdened with need and perplexity. "How long shall mine enemy be exalted over me?", asked David, Psa. 13.2; "O God, how long shall the enemy reproach?", asked Asaph, 74.10; "Lord, how long shall the wicked, how long shall the wicked triumph? How long shall they utter and speak hard things? and all the workers of iniquity boast themselves?", 94.4. In the future, martyrs prior to their resurrection will cry, "How long, O Lord, holy and true, dost thou not judge and avenge our blood on them that dwell on the earth?", Rev. 6.10.

14   The other saint or holy one knew the answer: 2,300 days. This is seven months short of seven years, so cannot refer directly to the whole of the 70th week yet to come. Of course, such an answer will give courage to those who have to suffer in the future great tribulation. But remember that this answer concludes the **vision**, not the **interpretation** of the vision. So it need not be symbolic nor futuristic. It would therefore seem to refer to the period before the temple was cleansed by Judas Maccabees in B.C. 165. In other words, divine truth will ultimately conquer and prevail.

The Distinctive Interpretation of the Vision, 8.15-27

15   The meaning of the vision was not granted immediately to Daniel, neither could he have any recourse to the methods of the Chaldeans. A heavenly vision needs a heavenly interpretation; spiritual things are spiritually discerned through what the Holy Spirit teaches, 1 Cor. 2.13,14. One with the "appearance of a man" stood before Daniel having the authority to give commands to Gabriel; in Luke 1.26 only God has the authority to give commands to Gabriel, so we conclude that this One who appeared to Daniel was the Lord in one of His pre-incarnation appearances. In these verses, the language of heaven was the language that Daniel understood; in 1 Corinthians 13.1 the "tongues . . . of angels" were not strange utterances not understood without an interpreter, but angels speaking in languages (not their own) understood by men. There is no record of a voice from heaven, meant to be understood by men, yet in a language not comprehensible to the men being addressed. (John 12.28-30 is no exception; the voice of the Father was addressed to the Son, not to men who merely heard a thunder.)

16   The divine voice above the waters was in command, far above the affairs of earth. Thus in Genesis 1, the voice was far beyond what was being created; in Exodus 20, the voice on Sinai was far beyond the mere camp of men below; the voice from the mercy seat in the tabernacle stood far beyond and removed from Moses and Aaron who were addressed. The command "Gabriel, make this man to understand the vision" shows that Daniel, now very old, was still teachable as in chapter 1 when he was very young. Gabriel, meaning "man of God, God is mighty," also appears in 9.21 to give understanding of the future, and in Luke 1.19,26 telling of the forthcoming birth of John the Baptist and of the Lord Jesus, as well as of His eternal kingdom. Gabriel was a heavenly messenger to communicate the divine mind regarding future events. (The archangel Michael, the only archangel named as such in Scripture, is seen in Daniel 10.13; 12.1, where he protects God's people, in Jude 9 where he appears to be protecting Moses' body, and in Revelation 12.7 where he protects the sanctity of heaven by casting out Satan into the earth. He may be the archangel at the rapture, 1 Thess. 4.16.) In passing, we should state that the name Gabriel appears in the non-canonical writings, as the book of Enoch.

17 There was no "worshipping of angels," Col. 1.18, when Daniel fell before Gabriel. Rather it was an act of fear that caused him to fall on his face. This fear was (i) his personal fear before the strange appearance of the Man and Gabriel, and (ii) his fear as to what was to happen to his people the Jews. The vision of the ram and the goat referred to "the time of the end," not just to the two kingdoms from which the vision was derived. We ourselves must understand this correctly, in just the same way as Daniel was exhorted to "understand." The kingdoms of Medo-Persia and Greece do not stretch to the end; we have seen in chapters 2 and 7 that the iron-clay kingdom and the kingdom of the fourth beast stretch to the end times. Rather it is the "little horn" of 8.9 that is used symbolically to denote features of the end times, demonstrating religious and military enmity against God's people. As the king of the north, he comes to his end in Daniel 11.45.

18 Daniel was in a very special state of mind—unlike that of Nebuchadnezzar in chapter 2 when he had an ordinary dream during normal sleep. The fall had produced the "deep sleep" in Daniel; yet he was conscious of the voice although feeling a sense of deep physical weakness. His physical posture was continued into the dream—the touch to set him upright was something personally appreciated in the dream; no doubt he lay on the ground physically all the time until he awoke. And when he awoke, he promptly fainted and was ill for several days, v.27, suggesting a state of shock in his old age. See also 10.8,9, where there was no strength in Daniel, and when he lay in a deep sleep on the ground although appreciating voices speaking to him. In Luke 1, when Gabriel spoke to Zacharias and Mary, no special mental state is described, but in Acts 10.10, Peter was hungry and fell into a trance, when ordinary consciousness ceased so that the soul should be aware only of a revelation from heaven. God used special means to communicate with special people at special times requiring great revelation. In the N.T., there is no indication that God used these means quite generally, nor that He uses them today. The quotation in Acts 2.17 refers to matters still future, "in the last days," and it was not quoted by Peter to refer to the day of Pentecost.

19 Gabriel commenced by mentioning "the last end of the indignation," referring to the finality of God's righteous wrath. The "end" will be according to God's timetable, and will be introduced in His time. Men's plans, good or bad, will not take God's timetable into account, and men will continue to plan "beyond the end," but God's time can never be altered, in just the same way as "the hour" of the Lord's death could be neither advanced nor retarded by men's activity (for example, it was impossible for the Lord to die at the time of John 8.59; 10.31.) Many times in Matthew 24 we read of the "end," namely the coming of the Lord in power and glory.

There was, of course, another "end" to the prophecy in Daniel 8, namely the termination of the activity of Antiochus Epiphanes, and this duplication of meaning is characteristic of prophecy—a local meaning referring to the near future as far as Daniel was concerned, and what is still future as far as we are concerned even now. So Daniel's vision was **historical** (from our view point) in the time of the third beast, referring to Antiochus. But the vision was also far-distant **prophetical**, still future and to occur in the time of the fourth beast, enabling the reader to perceive both religious enmity in the person of the anti-Christ, and military enmity in the person of the king of the north. God uses one event in history to foreshadow another; both were future for Daniel, but for us one is long since past. The same phenomenon appears in chapter 9, where 70 years of local history are projected to 70 weeks of future history. Similarly in Matthew 24; the destruction of the temple in A.D.70 widens out to the circumstances surrounding "the end of the world," Matt. 24.2,3.

20 As already explained, the ram denotes the kings of Media and Persia. The "two horns" stand for Darius and Cyrus, the latter being greater as seen in verse 3. The ram denoted all the kings down to the collapse of the empire.

21 Unlike what is given in verse 7, the overthrow of the second kingdom is not explained here, but the goat stands for the succession of kings over the empire of Greece. The "great horn" was the "first king," known historically to have been Alexander the Great. His name is not predicted in Scripture, unlike that of Cyrus which was predicted by Isaiah long beforehand, Isa. 44.28.

22 There is now described the immediate degeneracy of the third kingdom. In his relatively early age, Alexander died and had no successor, so the unity was broken, and the whole kingdom was divided into four parts, each under the control of a general; see verse 8. Gabriel added that these four generals would be "not in his power," namely not having the power of Alexander. Throughout history, including recent times, the power of an archdictator cannot be matched afterwards— except, of course, at the end, when the power of the last beast will be replaced by the infinite power of the Lord Jesus reigning in His kingdom.

23 As verse 8 passes on to verse 9, so verse 22 passes on to verse 23; predicted history passes on from B.C. 323 (the death of Alexander) to B.C. 176 (when Antiochus Epiphanes became king of Syria). From now on, the "king of fierce countenance" refers not only to Antiochus, but much more to the king of the north of the end times, the former in his military exploits being a type of the latter. He will be defiant of all moral principles and in his attitude to God. He will "understand dark sentences." This is the same word as used in Samson's *riddle*, Jud. 14.12, and the *hard questions* of the queen of Sheba, 1 Kings 10.1; see Psalm 78.2; Matt. 13.35. But more specifically, God stated that He would speak to Moses mouth to mouth (with comprehension), and not in *dark speeches*, Num. 12.8. The king's activity is the opposite to this; God did not expect Moses to understand dark speeches, and quite generally, the Lord is the true Revealer, since in Him "are hid all the treasures of wisdom and knowledge," Col. 2.3. The king's ability, then, must be Satanically motivated, for no doubt he will understand the most secret things of science (with discoveries kept secret by the governments of the world) together with their destructive power in warfare. This power is similarly seen in the second beast in Revelation 13, where there will be wonders, fire from heaven, deception, with life being given to the image, vs. 13-15.

The idea behind "the transgressors" coming to the full appears to refer to Israel's guilt in that coming day; the enemy will direct his power against them as well as against any faithful remnant.

24   Gabriel then announced the origin of the power of this king. In the case of the Lord Jesus, Peter stated that His works were those "which God did by him," Acts 2.22; the Lord declared that His works were those "which the Father hath given me," John 5.36; it was the Spirit who anointed Him to preach, Luke 4.18. How this contrasts with the origin of the power of this king of fierce countenance; it will be "not by his own power," and will therefore be Satanic. This applies to other great personages of this future age. The beast that ascends "out of the bottomless pit," Rev. 11.7, will bring Satanic power with him; the anti-Christ as the man of sin will be characterized by "the working of Satan with all power," 2 Thess. 2.9. As the Spirit was upon God's Leader in the days of His flesh, so will Satan be upon his leaders in the coming day.

The king will "prosper," namely for self. And he will "destroy" (i) what is of God, the Jews as "the holy people," and (ii) the "mighty" (a word in the plural—the mighty ones) no doubt referring to the nations. We find both of these in Daniel 11.41,42, "the glorious land" and "the countries."

25   To cause "craft to prosper" suggests that the means of warfare will be prosecuted by the development of sophisticated weapons. In the case of the anti-Christ, such craft would be necessary for the "great wonders" and for the means of deceiving the people, Rev. 13.13,14. In fact, all the great personages in power at the end time will enhance their ambitions by these means. Additionally, this king of the north "shall magnify himself in his heart" like Nebuchadnezzar before him, Dan. 4.30, and Satan also, Isa. 14.23; anti-Christ too will exalt himself "above all that is called God," 2 Thess. 2.4. Moreover, this king of fierce countenance "by peace shall destroy many"—namely, "in security shall destroy many"; there will be no opposition to stop his activity. By fighting against Israel, the king will also stand up against "the Prince of princes"—the King of kings and the Lord of lords. He seems to be confederate with the anti-Christ; their combined activity against the true God will be totally on a greater scale similar to what Antiochus did in Jerusalem and its temple. Also the beast with the nations shall fight against the Lamb at the end of that period, Rev. 17.14, fulfilling the psalm of David, "the kings of the earth set themselves . . . against the Lord, and against his anointed," Psa. 2.2.

But this king "shall be broken without hand." In Revelation 19.20, the beast and the false prophet are cast by divine means into the lake of fire—no men or nations will be used to achieve this end. And the same with the king of the north; God will not use any human agency to cut off his life and activity. This is unlike Mystery Babylon, corrupt Christendom at its absolute zenith, when God will use the beast and the ten kings to destroy her absolutely so that "Babylon is fallen," 17.14-18.

26 The second part of the vision now comes to an end. Gabriel expressed the certainty of the vision and its interpretation by stating that it was "true." The reference to the "evening and the morning" appears to derive from the fact that the vision was divided into two parts, vs. 3-14; 18-25, the former taking part in the evening (the beginning of the complete period known as the day), and the second part in the morning following. Thus Daniel "sought for the meaning," v.15, during the time between the evening and the morning, so this was not just a mere fleeting exercise.

The vision was to be "shut up": not to be hidden so that no one could read it or understand it, but to be preserved for all future readers, even "for many days." Readers would know when the appointed time had come, in the days of Antiochus Epiphanes, and more particularly in the time of the anti-Christ and the king of the north, all reaching far beyond Daniel's time. The same may be said about Daniel 12.9, where we read of words "closed up and sealed till the time of the end."

27 The old man was exhausted, and ill for several days, suffering on behalf of his people who would pass through such tribulation in the last days. Compare this with Paul, who was ill with anxiety on behalf of the Corinthians, 2 Cor. 1.3-11; 7.5-7, and with the Lord Jesus who wept as He saw and contemplated the sorrows of others, John 11.33-35, Luke 19.41-44.

Although Daniel had the interpretation of the first part of the vision it may be that he did not fully understand it—"none understood it." The prophets in the O.T. searched, but could not fully understand, 1 Pet. 1.11. We have more understanding now, since we have the complete Scriptures relating to the Person of Christ and to all prophetical matters. Concerning the prophecy of Daniel, the Lord said, "whoso readeth, let him understand," Matt. 24.15; in other words, the details of Daniel should **not now** be beyond the understanding of those who have the whole of Scripture in their hands and hearts. We should search the Scriptures daily, as they did in Berea, Acts 17.11, having "a more sure word of prophecy" in the written Word of God, that is of no "private interpretation," 2 Pet. 1.19-21.

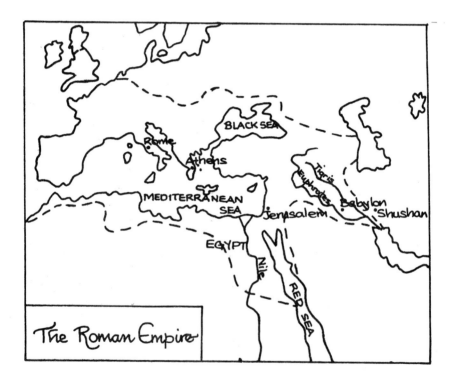

The Roman Empire

Chapter 9
Daniel's Intercession and the Vision
of the Seventy Weeks

Context of the Chapter, 9.1-3

1   Daniel is now found in the new kingdom of the Medo-Persians. "Darius the Mede took the kingdom," 5.31, after which there had been the episode of the lion's den, ch. 6. Chapter 9 took place still in the first year of Darius, before Cyrus the Persian became ruler over the united empire, 1.21. These were the two horns of the ram, 8.3, one higher than the other, the higher one (Cyrus) coming up last. Our verse states that Darius "was made king"—strictly by God who sets kings up and sets them down.

2   In the first year, Daniel had understanding of remarks made by Jeremiah many years previously; he gained his information from "books," or "letters" as the word is often translated. Clearly this refers to what we know as the book of the prophecy of Jeremiah. Daniel may well have had a copy of the whole of the O.T. as was then written, for someone must have preserved God's Word throughout the period of the captivity. In particular, Daniel knew about the 70 years that Jeremiah had prophesied concerning "the desolations of Jerusalem." For example, Jeremiah had written a letter from Jerusalem to the people of the captivity in Babylon, Jer. 29.1, telling them of the predicted length of their captivity, "after seventy years be accomplished at Babylon I will visit you, and perform my good word toward you, in causing you to return to this place," v.10. So Daniel must have known Jeremiah's words very well (without chapter and verse numbers for ease of location), and he trusted in these predictions.

As a whole, Jeremiah had been written by Baruch at Jeremiah's dictation, Jer. 36.4,18. This had been read in the Lord's house, vs. 8,10, and before the princes in the king's house, v.15. Then it had been read before the king by Jehudi, v.21, but after the reading of "three or four leaves," it had been cut and burnt by the king, v.23, who showed no fear at such a savage attack on God's Word. It had then been rewritten by Baruch, with extra material added, v.32. So the original roll, or a copy, or selected portions of it, had been possessed by Daniel 70 years later.

There are other references to these 70 years in the O.T. "I will take away from them . . . the voice of the bridegroom, and the voice of the bride . . . this whole land shall be a desolation . . . these nations shall serve the king of Babylon seventy years . . . When seventy years are accomplished, I will punish the king of Babylon, and that nation . . . for their iniquity," Jer. 25.10-12. Historically, we see this fulfilled in 2 Chronicles 36.21,22; the land kept its sabbaths for 70 years, after which "the Lord stirred up the spirit of Cyrus king of Persia" to ensure that men returned to Jerusalem to rebuild the house of the Lord; see Ezra 1.1. In the second year of Darius, Zechariah had a vision, in which an angel asked how long the Lord would not have mercy on Jerusalem that had been wasted for 70 years, Zech. 1.12. In Zechariah 7.4-7, the prophet had to complain about the activity of the priests during these 70 years: they were acting for themselves and not for God.

Yet at the end of these 70 years, Daniel could see no difference in the nation's circumstances, although the time had apparently arrived. In the reign of Darius, Cyrus was not yet on the throne as the one who could order the rebuilding of the temple. If Daniel knew Isaiah 44.27,28, he must have been waiting for Cyrus to take the throne! Hence he knew that there must be special repentance and intercession on behalf of the nation before God, and Daniel 9 is occupied with this—a great plea for the nation and for Jerusalem. He was thereby fulfilling the command of God through Moses; returning unto the Lord and obedience to His voice would lead to the return of the captivity, Deut. 30.1-3. After the return, Ezra made a great confession before the Lord, Ezra 9.5, as likewise did the Levites in Nehemiah 9.

The reason why the length of the captivity was 70 years is not hard to ascertain. In Leviticus 25.4, every seventh year was to be a sabbath unto the land, during which year there was to be no food production from the land. If the children of Israel disregarded this commandment, 26.31-35 would follow; the nation would be scattered with the land desolate, so "shall the land enjoy her sabbaths, as long as it lieth desolate." Now the duration of the Jewish monarchy from the selection of Saul to be king up to the beginning of the captivity was 490 years, and the disregard of God's commandment would mean that 70 land-sabbath years were misused over that period. These 70 years were turned into captivity for the people and for the desolation of the land; "then shall the land rest, and enjoy her sabbaths," v.34. The people had to restore what had been taken away. So 490 years of the monarchy gave rise to 70 years of captivity, while in Daniel 9.24, 70 weeks give rise to 490 years of prophecy, (483 ending with the last week of Messiah on earth, and the final 7 taking place after the rapture). The similarity in these two sets of numbers is remarkable, and not without significance!

3 Preparation for prayer involved setting the face "unto the Lord God," as in 6.10 where he set his face toward Jerusalem, towards the place where God had once dwelt—towards the mount of Olives where the glory had departed. For Daniel, this kind of prayer was a continual activity, "continuing instant in prayer," Rom. 12.12. At the same time, Daniel took the lowest physical position. He engaged in fasting, effectively as in 1.8, and in 10.3. Many fasted for particular reasons, such as Ezra and his company, Ezra 8.23; Israel in sackcloth, Neh. 9.1; Paul and other teachers in Antioch, Acts 13.3, while the Lord Himself fasted for forty days in the wilderness, Matt. 4.2. In "sackcloth, and ashes" implied the worthlessness of self, as Mordecai, Esther 4.1. Daniel was far removed from the hypocritical self-glorification of those who disfigured their faces and appeared as fasting to men, Matt. 6.26; such men have their reward now in this life!

Confession Precedes Prayer, 9.4-15

4 The order is significant; Daniel's confession preceded his prayer in verses 16-19. This confession and prayer could be to none other save the Lord God. It is so in N.T. times, whatever some religious people may do today. The Lord Jesus is the one way of approach, whatever tradition and religious edicts demand in some circles, where men, alive and dead, are supposed to stand between man and God. But Daniel said directly, "the Lord *my* God." After that he said, *"our* God," vs.9,10,13,14,15,17. He finally reverts to *"my* God," vs. 18,19. This shows that his prayer was very personal, yet he was speaking on behalf of his nation burdened under the rigours of the captivity. Such a personal appreciation was expressed by Paul when he wrote, *"my* God shall supply," Phil. 4.19, and by Thomas, who confessed, *"my* Lord, and *my* God," John 20.28. Moreover, the title "the great and dreadful God" is how Daniel viewed God in relationship to the law, meting out cursing or blessing. Certainly this title has no "Father" character about it.

The mention of "the covenant," and the reference to mercy shown "to them that love him, and to those that keep his commandments," take our minds back to Exodus 20.6 when the ten commandments were first given. Daniel appears to be quoting Deuteronomy 7.9, where Moses was expanding upon the necessity of keeping the commandments. This shows that Daniel was well acquainted with the Pentateuch, as well as the prophets, and we may believe that he possessed a copy of the O.T. Scriptures. This covenant was a "two-party" covenant, involving God's side in His mercy, and man's side in keeping the commandments—unlike the new covenant which is a "one-party" covenant involving God's mercy alone.

5 Daniel stressed that there had been a two-fold disobedience, (i) to the Word of God, v.5, and (ii) to the prophets, v.6.

Daniel used several words in verse 5 to describe this disobedience.
(i) **Sin**, meaning to err or to miss the mark, namely to deviate at an angle
from the original straight path. (ii) **Iniquity,** meaning to waver, involving a variety of sinful directions forming no overall policy.
(iii) **Wickedness,** the outworking of a pathway of rebellion.
(iv) **Rebellion,** involving knowledge of the truth, but a deliberate act of
turning backwards by "departing." This may be seen in 2 Kings 17.13,14
where necks were hardened at the commandments, and in 2 Chronicles
36.13 where king Zedekiah refused to turn to the Lord God. Originally,
the people had been self-confident that they could keep the law, Exod.
19.8, even before they knew its contents. So often it was the breaking of
the first commandment that led the people into conflict with God, into
trouble and judgment—this was manifested by idolatry, in the temple in
Jerusalem, and elsewhere in the northern kingdom, 1 Kings 17.35-41;
2 Chron. 28.22-25.

6   In Exodus 20, God spoke directly to the fearful people, but
     usually He spoke through His servants and prophets. By stating
"*thy* servants" and "in *thy* name," Daniel implied the divine authority
behind what was spoken. As in verse 8, all classes of society were addressed by God's servants: "kings, princes, fathers, people," showing the
widespread distribution of the spoken word. In fact, the leaders of a
nation are often responsible for its decay. For example, consider the prophecy of Jeremiah, and note how often the prophet spoke to kings, as
well as unto the people. Paul too would carry the Name of Christ to
kings and to the people, Acts 9.15. However, the preached word is not
just for leaders—it is for "all the people," and the same may be said of
any local church today. Yet Daniel's confession was that all classes of
society had not hearkened; God sent messengers, "but they mocked the
messengers of God, and despised his words, and misused his prophets,"
2 Chron. 36.15,16; Matt. 21.34-36.

7   Here we have several positive and negative assertions regarding
     God and the people. To the Lord, "righteousness belongeth,"
namely in judgment as in verse 14. Could any think that God's judgment
is otherwise? "Thou art righteous, O Lord . . . because thou hast judged
thus," Rev. 16.5; "true and righteous are his judgments," 19.2; "him that
judgeth righteously," 1 Pet. 2.23. This contrasts with the state of men on
earth, "all our righteousnesses are as filthy rags," Isa. 64.6. No wonder
Daniel's nation manifested "confusion of faces"—unable to look God
straight in the face, and hence quite unlike Moses whom God knew face
to face, Deut. 34.10.

Daniel embraced both the southern and northern kingdoms. Those
"near" were the Jewish captives in Babylon, from Jerusalem and the
southern kingdom; by contrast those "far off" related to the northern

kingdom, having been taken captive by the Assyrians about 180 years previously, 2 Kings 17.5,23. By saying "where *thou* hast driven them," he was recalling verses such as "*the Lord* . . . removed them out of his sight," and "*the Lord* removed Israel out of his sight," 2 Kings 17.18,23, in keeping with the words of Solomon, "If . . . *thou* . . . deliver them to the enemy," 1 Kings 8.46.

8 By stating again this list of men judged, Daniel implied that divine judgment is no respecter of persons. Kings were the overall leaders and ultimately responsible; princes were rulers over provinces; fathers were rulers over families; "we" stood for the common people, who were also responsible before God. Today, church leaders, such as elders, often lead the Lord's people astray in doctrine and in practice, as Paul could foresee when he addressed the Ephesian elders in Acts 20.29,30.

9 Before continuing this theme, Daniel presented the contrast between God's mercy in the past and the people's rebellion. Such mercy is often found in the Books of the Judges and Kings, when God saved His people from the invading nations. When Solomon dedicated the temple, he knew God's forgiveness from the past, and he anticipated it again in the future; he **commenced** by saying "when thou hearest, forgive," 1 Kings 8.30, and he **concluded** with "forgive thy people that have sinned against thee," v.50. In between, Solomon visualized many aspects of sin, concluding with the confession "We have sinned . . . in the land of their enemies, which led them away captive," vs. 47,48. Daniel was, in effect, re-echoing Solomon's prayer.

10 By recognizing the act of disobedience, Daniel quickly returned to the confession of sin. In the O.T. under law, obedience **would lead** to life; in the N.T. under grace, obedience **follows** from eternal life possessed by the believer. Before the details of the law had been given, blessings were promised under the condition "if ye will obey my voice," Exod. 19.5. The people stated that they would do the commands of God, **before** these were given, and **afterwards** as well, v. 8; 24.3. These commands had been set forth by God's "servants the prophets." Moses was such a prophet, after whom none arose in Israel like him "whom the Lord knew face to face," Deut. 34.10; generally speaking, it was by the prophets that God had spoken in the O.T., Heb. 1.1. They often recalled the law, amplified it, interpreted it and applied it. In the N.T., God had spoken by His Son, and then through His apostles and prophets; today He uses His Word, as spiritually expounded by teachers placed amongst the local churches.

11 But Daniel rehearsed the complete departure from the revealed law and voice of God. The fact that the people had not obeyed the voice of God appears more than ten times in Jeremiah. Concerning

Moses, Stephen recalled, "to whom our fathers would not obey, but thrust him from them," Acts 7.39. All this disobedience arose from one source, "by one man's disobedience many were made sinners," Rom. 5.19, causing the wrath of God to fall on "the children of disobedience," Eph. 5.6.

Daniel knew that this was the reason why "the curse is poured upon us," a curse being the opposite to blessing. Moses had foreseen this, and had warned the people prior to the crossing of Jordan: "a blessing, if ye obey the commandments . . . a curse, if ye will not obey the commandments of the Lord your God, but turn aside . . . to go after other gods, whom ye have not known," Deut. 11.27,28. Chapter 28 is devoted to blessings for obedience, and curses and plagues for disobedience, "because thou wouldest not obey the voice of the Lord," v.62. The curses are set forth in verses 15-68, and Daniel must have known these details. God had foretold, "therefore shalt thou serve thine enemies which the Lord shall send against thee," v.48; "ye shall be plucked from off the land whither thou goest to possess it," v.63; "the Lord shall scatter thee among all people," v.64, and all this took place in the Assyrian and Babylonian captivities.

12 What God had foretold will ultimately come to pass, and so the Babylonian captivity "confirmed" God's warnings spoken centuries before. And it is the same for the future: God has "appointed a day, in the which he will judge the world in righteousness," Acts 17.31. Men could not escape judgment in the O.T., and neither can men today if they "neglect so great salvation," Heb. 2.3.

The 'judges" referred to cannot be only the judges raised up after Joshua to deliver the nation from constant invading hordes from surrounding territory; rather they would refer to the leaders of the nation, so often being responsible for leading the nation down the sinful path.

Daniel then stressed the uniqueness of the destruction of Jerusalem, "for under the whole heaven hath not been done as hath been done upon Jerusalem." This had involved the complete destruction of the capital city where God had dwelt. The news of its destruction did not reach the captives until 20 years after the captivity began, Ezek. 35.21. Previously this city had been unique in the opposite sense, "Beautiful for situation, the joy of the whole earth," Psa. 48.2, but in Daniel's day a passer-by might say, "Is this the city that men call The perfection of beauty, The joy of the whole earth?" Lam. 2.15. Its punishment had been greater than the punishment of the sin of Sodom, 4.6. And in the future, Jerusalem will be the centre of the unique great tribulation, "a time of trouble, such as never was . . . even to that same time," Dan. 12.1. Jerusalem has been, and always will be, unique, a centre of discord amongst the nations until Messiah's kingdom arrives. By present-day standards, Jerusalem was certainly not the largest city to fall and to be destroyed in warfare—that distinction belongs to Berlin in 1945. But in the O.T., Jerusalem had that distinction, brought about by the intervention of God. Again, in Exodus 34.10, God claimed that His intervention in driving out the heathen tribes was unique, "I will do marvels, such as have not been done in all the earth, nor in any nation."

13   The law should have been an adequate warning, but the Jews took no heed (particularly in the light of what had previously happened to the northern kingdom). There had been no prayer, the exercise of which might have turned those exercised from iniquity to the truth. Sin blinds the minds of men, and prayer seems irrelevant and unnecessary. The proper course should be, "Pray that ye enter not into temptation," as the Lord said, Luke 22.40; "I pray to God that ye do no evil," as Paul wrote, 2 Cor. 13.7. So long after the event, Daniel was seeking to make up for this deficiency.

14   From the time of Moses up to Nebuchadnezzar was about 900 years, and during all this period "the Lord watched upon the evil." The word "evil" refers to the desolations of Jerusalem, as verses 12 and 13 show. God "watched" upon this in the sense that during the 900 years, He knew that He would have to bring it to pass; likewise He watched upon the evil during the 70 years captivity, knowing that it had to take its course until this period was completed. In fact, during the 900 years in which the people often departed from the law, the necessity of judgment was ever before Him, causing Him to visit judgment upon the nation on many occasions. He also watched upon mercy, and this was interspersed with judgment, as, for example, in the days of the judges. Throughout, God was "righteous" in His acts of judgment; it could not have been otherwise, for the results of judgment were, and are, always consistent with His righteousness. Thus Paul wrote of the "revelation of the righteous judgment of God" against unbelievers, Rom. 2.5; 2 Thess. 1.5, and of "the Lord, the righteous judge" pertaining to believers, 2 Tim. 4.8. Peter wrote that the Lord Jesus "committed himself to him that judgeth righteously," 1 Pet. 2.23; while a voice from the altar said, "true and righteous are thy judgments" when the seven bowls were being poured out, Rev. 16.7.

15   Daniel finally confessed the sin of the nation to the One (i) who had brought the nation out of Egypt, and (ii) who had obtained "renown" before the nations around. This renown had caused the nations to know "my fear," Exod. 23.27; Rahab confessed the testimony of this renown to the two spies, Josh. 2.9-11. In the Lord's lifetime on earth, this renown is called "fame" in Luke 4.37, "the fame of him went out into every place of the country round about."

Prayer Follows Confession, 9.16-19

16 Prayer without confession and repentance will not get very far. But Daniel adopted the spiritual order, and now with his own heart cleared he can turn to prayer, using the titles "Lord; our God; my God." Daniel desired that the nations no longer rejoice over the destruction of Jerusalem, by God turning from His anger and fury. It would be on the grounds of "righteousness" that God's judgment would cease, in just the same way as it had been on these grounds that it had commenced. It is on the grounds of righteousness that He now acts towards us in salvation, Rom. 3.21.

In these verses, note that Daniel stresses the idea of God's possessions: "*thy* city Jerusalem; *thy* holy mountain; *thy* people; *thy* servant; *thy* sanctuary." How this holy thought of possession is found so often in the Psalms and the prophets; the city and Zion are an oft-recurring thought. The "city of God" appears four times in the Psalms; for example, "Glorious things are spoken of thee, O city of God," Psa. 87.3. "My holy mountain" is found six times in Isaiah; for example, "They shall not hurt nor destroy in all my holy mountain," Isa. 11.9. Today, we should stress that the church is God's church; for example, "the church of God which is at Corinth," 1 Cor. 1.2. Christians do not possess the church (namely, the company of believers) in which God has placed them.

Daniel recalled that Jerusalem and its one-time inhabitants had become "a reproach to all that are about us." Namely, they had become a disgrace in testimony, having lost status, distinction, power, separation and beauty. The nations round about would laugh at the thought that this had once been the place of God's choice; "We are become a reproach to our neighbours, a scorn and derision to them that are round about us," said Asaph, Psa. 79.4.

17 In the light of all this, Daniel said, "therefore." This prayer after confession forms a logical ordering; faith that confesses sin has a greater certainty when prayer rightly follows. The two aspects go together, as in Luke 18.13 where the publican expressed confession and prayer in the same sentence; the result was immediate, for he went to his house justified.

Daniel cried "hear" in the three verses 17,18,19. It reminds us of Solomon's words: "hear" when prayer is made in the temple or towards it, 2 Chron. 6.23,25,27,30,33,35,39, with God's ears "attent unto the prayer that is made in this place," v.40.

Daniel prayed that God's face would shine "upon the sanctuary that is desolate." Many years before, this shining of glory had departed to the mount of Olives, Ezek. 11.23. Daniel desired its return, since Jerusalem was still the place of God's choice—it was still in God's prophetic program. This exercise that God should shine often appears in the O.T. Asaph cried "shine forth" in Psalm 80.1,3,7,19 in a day when there was no open vision; in Psalm 94.1 marg., "shine forth" relates to judgment. Admittedly, the glory of God was not seen on earth again until the birth of the Lord Jesus, Luke 2.9, and will not be seen again until the glory returns from the east (the mount of Olives) to the restored house, Ezek. 43.4.

18 Daniel, at the end of the 70 years, believed that if God would just look at the desolations wrought upon Jerusalem, then in mercy He would allow the rebuilding of the city. This could never be on the ground of the "righteousnesses" of the Jews, but it would be based entirely on God's mercy. Daniel recalled that the city was called by God's *Name*, and hence it was so important to rebuild what was associated so closely with God. For example, it was "The city *of the Lord*," Isa. 60.14; "the city *of God*," Psa. 46.4; "the city *of the great King*," Psa. 48.2; Matt. 5.35; "the city *of the living God*" (spiritually), Heb. 12.22.

Daniel seemed to have certainty that his prayer would be answered. In the N.T., conditions for prayers to be answered are many and varied. Prayer must be characterized by: a good thing asked, Matt. 7.11; two agreeing on earth,18.19; faith without doubting, 21.21; believing that the thing asked will come to pass, Mark 11.22,23; "If ye had faith," Luke 17.6; asking in His Name, John 14.13; abiding in Christ with His words abiding in us, 15.7; not asking amiss, James 4.3; the prayer of a righteous man, 5.16; keeping His commandments and doing things pleasing in His sight, 1 John 3.22; asking "according to his will," 5.14.

19 This verse represents Daniel's final desperate pleadings: "forgive, hearken, defer not, do." In other words, "act now" since the 70 years of captivity are complete. Although Daniel used the title *"my* God," he did not say "my Lord." The word "Lord" used here is not *Jehovah*, but *Adonai*, showing the speaker's inadequacy and God's limitless sovereignty and infinite resources, as in Psalm 40.17. In the O.T., there are only a very few occasions where "my" is used before Adonai: Exod. 4.10; Jud. 6.15; Isa. 49.14. But Daniel used the description *"thy* city . . . *thy* people," asking the Lord to restore His own possessions; contrast this with verse 24, where *"thy* people . . . *thy* holy city" refer to Daniel's possessions, namely what occupied his heart so much before God.

The Immediate Answer, 9.20-23

20 What a blessed truth appears in this verse! God begins to answer even while the prayer is in progress! The whole verse is occupied with this—"*whiles* I was speaking, and praying and confessing . . . and presenting . . . yea, *whiles* I was speaking in prayer . . . ." In other words, the prayer was not only heard, but God commenced to act *during* the prayer. This is seen in verse 23, where Gabriel said, *"At the beginning of thy supplications the commandment came forth . . . ."* That is to say, *during* the double confession (for Daniel's sin, and for the people's sin), and *during* the supplication for the "*holy* mountain" where the temple had been in Jerusalem, God's mercy commenced to be manifest. Indeed Jerusalem had been characterized by the great truth expressed by Solomon, "the places are *holy*, whereunto the ark of the Lord is come," 2 Chron. 8.11. The future reign of peace will ensure that in God's "*holy* mountain" there shall be no hurt nor destruction, Isa. 65.25.

We recall that Abraham's servant prayed as he came to the city of Nahor in Mesopotamia, asking that success might come to his mission in seeking out a bride for Isaac. How did God answer?—"*before* he had done speaking . . . Rebekah came out," Gen. 24.12-15. For God has promised, "*before* they call, I will answer; and *while* they are yet speaking, I will hear," Isa. 65.24. And yet there is the other side to the divine response. When Nebuchadnezzar was boasting to himself about his achievements in Babylon, "*While* the word was in the king's mouth, there fell a voice from heaven," Dan. 4.30,31.

21 The angel Gabriel (one of the two named angels in Scripture) had already appeared in 8.16 in the last year of Belshazzar and the Babylonian kingdom. Here he appears shortly afterwards in the first year of Darius and the Medo-Persian empire. He was caused "to fly swiftly," evidently from service elsewhere so as to interrupt Daniel in prayer—while he was speaking in prayer. We recall the heavenly interruption when the Lord Jesus was praying, when the Holy Spirit descended upon Him, Luke 3.21,22; when the falling of the Spirit interrupted Peter's preaching, Acts 10.44; and when the damsel Rhoda interrupted a prayer meeting with news about Peter's release from prison, Acts 12.14.

Gabriel's next named appearance was over 500 years later when he appeared to Elizabeth and Mary, to predict the births of John the Baptist and the Lord Jesus, Luke 1.19,26.

Daniel had been praying until "the time of the evening oblation"; this refers to the offering of the lamb every evening, Exod. 29.39, an offering that was made continually until the destruction of the temple by Nebuchadnezzar. Since that time, during the desolations of Jerusalem, there had been no such offering, for there was no temple and no altar: "The Lord hath cast off his altar," Lam. 2.7. Nevertheless, the remembrance of these offerings was still precious to Daniel after 70 years since leaving Jerusalem, and he still reckoned the time of day by that event. (We believe that Paul adopted the same practice in Acts 20.16; his mention of "the day of Pentecost" was not to observe some religious event, but only to refer conveniently to a particular date, that once had been the fourth Jewish feast, and the day when the Spirit had been given.)

22 Daniel had possessed skill and understanding in wisdom and science from his youth, Dan. 1.4,17, this having been given by God. Thus Bezaleel had been filled with wisdom and understanding for the construction of the tabernacle, Exod. 31.3. In Daniel's case, at the end of his life, this "skill and understanding" was to comprehend the deep purpose of God relating to Messiah. The time scale of this purpose was to be the same as that in Daniel chapters 2 and 7, stretching throughout Gentile history. But the objective would be entirely different, for here is explained the cutting off of Messiah, 9.26, and the ultimate blessing of the Jewish people, v.24, at the end of the 70 weeks.

23 In verse 20, Daniel had said, *"whiles* I was speaking," but here Gabriel went further, saying *"At the beginning* of thy supplications." The immediate answer to Daniel's prayer was that *divine* intervention caused Gabriel to come forth at the commandment *from God.* How often Scripture testifies of this angelic work. Thus in the matter of enticing Ahab to battle, *the Lord* said to a spirit, "go out, and do even so," 2 Chron. 18.21; again, *"he* shall give his angels charge over thee," Psa. 91.11, while the angels are called "ministering spirits, *sent* forth," Heb. 1.14. Moreover, the Lord Jesus testified of the same truth; *the Father* would give more than twelve legions of angels, Matt. 26.53.

Gabriel called Daniel "greatly beloved." Many are called *beloved* in Scripture, and believers today come into the same category. For example, Solomon was declared to be "beloved of his God," Neh. 13.26; the church in Jerusalem called Barnabas and Paul "our beloved," Acts 15.25; Paul called the church in Rome "beloved of God," Rom. 1.7; Onesimus was named "a faithful and beloved brother," Col. 4.9. For Daniel, this was a title granted in his old age, accumulating from faithfulness over the years. Whereas we rejoice in such a title, it must be pointed out that the proper meaning of the word as applied to Daniel is "desirable"; we shall expand on this later in Daniel 10.11.

The Seventy Weeks Prophecy, 9.24-27

24 The Hebrew word here translated "weeks" is, throughout the O.T., usually translated "week" as demanded by the context, but the word means a group of seven, or a **heptad.** So we understand that the prophecy in this verse relates to 70 groups of 7, or 490 periods; the length of time involved in one period is, strictly speaking, not defined in the Book of Daniel. The prophet had been looking for the end of the 70 years, yet prophecy moved on instead to these 70 heptads. But in the Christian era, we now know things that Daniel did not know, and this enables us to ascertain the length of a period.

In verse 26, there are 69 weeks or heptads, involving 483 periods that must elapse before Messiah would be cut off; this would be the time between the command being given to rebuild the city up to the death of the Lord Jesus. It is not obvious which command in the O.T. is being alluded to. In fact, we read of three commands being given for building, but we must choose the right one.

(i) In Ezra 1.1-3, Cyrus gave the command to rebuild the temple; this took place in B.C. 536 at the end of the 70 years captivity, but since the rebuilding of the city was not involved, this cannot be the beginning of the 483 periods. (ii) In Ezra 6.3-8, we have a second decree by Darius for the completion of the building of the temple; this also cannot be the starting point. (iii) In Nehemiah 2.1-8 we find letters sent by king Artaxerxes for the rebuilding of the city, the date being B.C. 445.

This last command for the rebuilding of the city is the only date from which 483 periods can exist. Each period must equal one year, so a "week" in Daniel 9.24 must be understood as a week of years, namely seven years. This leaves the 70th week to be interpreted as 7 years according to the same reasoning. In fact, the calculation takes a year for a day (though it is impossible to apply this rule in every part of the O.T. as some have suggested!). For example, in Ezekiel 4.1-7, the prophet had to enact a symbolic siege for 430 days, "each day for a year," v.6. In Leviticus 25.8, a similar calculation is given, where "seven sabbaths of years" is stated to be 49 years. For the prophetic calculation in Daniel to be correct, leading up to the last week of the Lord's life on earth, (or to the day when He rode into Jerusalem in triumph, according to certain calculations), a year must be taken as 360 days. (Compare the figure 360 degrees associated with four right-angles embedded in ancient tradition.) The equality of three and a half years, 42 months, and 1,260 days, Rev. 11.2; 13.5; 11.3; 12.6, also shows that a prophetic year must be taken as 360 days.

The 70 weeks therefore denote 490 years, stretching up to the end of the times of the Gentiles, to the beginning of the fifth kingdom described in Daniel chs. 2,7. And this period is enlarged upon from the point of view of the Jews, rather than from that of the Gentiles. For Gabriel stated "thy people" and "thy holy city"; the nation would not yet be "my people," since they would remain "not my people" until these end times, Hosea 1.9; 2.23.

Six features of the end-time blessings are detailed by Gabriel:

(i) *"To finish the transgression."* In verse 5, Daniel had spoken of sin, iniquity and rebellion; apart from the faithful few at all times, this would continue up to the end times. Unbelief would characterize the nation in the intertestamental period, in the Christian era, and after the rapture of the Church. Ultimately, this state of sin will be concluded when they see the One whom they pierced, and when "all Israel shall be saved," Rom.

11.26, when God takes away their sins, v.27.

(ii) *"To make an end of sins."* This phrase marks an official end of a letter, marked with a seal so that there can be no starting again. Thus when a cheque is written out, a line is drawn after the amount of money stated in words, to indicate that no other writing can be inserted afterwards. After the Babylonian captivity, there was no more idolatry, but it was replaced by a formal system of Jewish religion; unbelieving men of this system crucified the Lord, and have remained in darkness ever since. But all this will come to an end when "they look upon me whom they have pierced," Zech. 12.10, and when they rest under the blessings of the new covenant, with their iniquities forgiven, and when their sin will be remembered no more, Jer. 31.31-34.

(iii) *"To make reconciliation for iniquity."* This word is usually translated "to make atonement" in the O.T., and properly means "to cover." The prophecy looks forward to the time when Israel will no longer be attached to the O.T. ceremony of atonement, but will find salvation fully in Christ. Only after "the fulness of the Gentiles" is come in, will the time come for the Deliverer to come to turn away ungodliness in Jacob, and when their sins will be taken away, Jer. 31.34; Rom. 11.26,27. The 490 years of sins involved will be forgiven in keeping with the 70 times 7 = 490 spoken of by the Lord relating to forgiveness, Matt. 18.22.

(iv) *"To bring in everlasting righteousness."* This is a millennial characteristic, deriving from the blood of Christ. After His crucifixion, Messiah had nothing, Dan. 9.26. But in that future day, Israel will no longer be seeking after righteousness according to the law, Rom. 9.31; 10.3, but will have "life from the dead," 11.15.

(v) *"To seal up the vision and prophecy."* In that millennial day, all judgment necessary to introduce the kingdom will have been concluded, so the prophetical word will be sealed in the sense that its forecasts of judgment will be closed and inoperative. The Word of God remains available, of course, but many of its predictions and their fulfilments will lie in the past when Messiah is reigning in glory.

(vi) *"To anoint the most Holy."* This cannot be to anoint the Lord! He is the anointed One, the Christ, Isa. 61.1; Luke 4.18; Acts 4.27; 10.38, not One yet to be anointed. Hence this phrase can only apply to a future most Holy place in God's dwelling, when His glory will anoint the holy temple into which He shall come, Ezek. 43.4-5; Mal. 3.1. This will not be a temple of types and shadows as in the O.T., but one for service with the Lord present.

25 The 70 weeks (490 years) leading up to these millennial blessings are here divided into 7 weeks (49 years), and 62 weeks (434 years), totalling 69 weeks (483 years). As already pointed out, the 70 weeks were not to commence in B.C. 536 as soon as the first captives returned to Jerusalem to rebuild the temple, 2 Chron. 36.23; Ezra 1.1-3. Rather it was B.C. 445, in the 20th year of Artaxerxes, when Nehemiah returned to rebuild the city walls, Neh. 2.1-11. There were then 483 prophetical years until the last week of the Lord Jesus prior to His death on the cross. Some expositors calculate that this period of years ended on the very day of the Lord's triumphant entry into Jerusalem, Matt. 21.10.

The initial 7 weeks (49 years) are separated from the rest, and would appear to refer to the time required for the complete rebuilding of the city of Jerusalem. It must be admitted that some theologians see nothing in these figures as leading up to the Lord Jesus; they are content merely to see profane history up to Antiochus Epiphanes.

26   After these 69 weeks (483 years), Messiah would be cut off, that is, in a sudden and cruel way, which we know was by crucifixion. The green tree, Luke 23.31, was cut down apparently without bearing any fruit, though men reckoned without the fruit of the travail of His soul bringing divine satisfaction, Isa. 53.11. This is what "but not for himself" means—"and shall have nothing." The Lord had entered Jerusalem as King but in His death there was no immediate outward show of a glorious kingdom. The object of the present vision is not to mention the kingdom of the Stone and of the Son of man, Dan. 2.45; 7.13,14, but to show the state of things leading up to it. It is not to declare a multitude of converts over the centuries, but to show that there is no outward kingdom for the Messiah until that great coming day.

After His crucifixion, in this vision no mention is made of the Church that commenced on the subsequent day of Pentecost. Rather, the city is in view, rebuilt in the Books of Ezra and Nehemiah, but after Messiah's death "the people of the prince that shall come shall destroy the city and the sanctuary." This occurred in A.D. 70, when the armies of Titus (emperor of the fourth kingdom) destroyed the city and Herod's temple.

The Lord predicted these events as well. Concerning **the city**, He said, "they shall not leave in thee one stone upon another" and "Jerusalem shall be trodden down of the Gentiles," Luke 19.44; 21.24. Concerning **the temple**, He said, "There shall not be left here one stone upon another," Matt. 24.2. So both Daniel and the Lord foretold this destruction, as did Stephen later, Acts 6.14. The "prince that shall come" does not refer particularly to Titus, since at this point the prophecy relating to A.D. 70 blends with the future end times, with the gap of the Church age passed over prophetically in silence. This "prince" will be the future leader of the fourth empire, the beast of Revelation 13.1. His "people" are the armies of the fourth kingdom, for example, as operating in A.D.70.

The future is linked with the past. "With a flood," or an overflow, indicates that Jerusalem has always been trodden down of the Gentiles. There shall be wars unto the end, for there shall be no peace for Jerusalem until the Prince of peace reigns, Isa. 9.6. "Desolations are determined" is a phrase declaring God's plan for the city that rejected Christ. There had been desolations for 70 years, Dan. 9.2, and in this prophecy there will be desolations again from A.D. 70 until the end times, for Jerusalem throughout this period is "a burdensome stone for all people," Zech. 12.3.

27 The "one week" in this verse corresponds to the 70th week (7 years) of this prophecy. It refers to the far future, after the rapture of the Church and prior to the millennial reign. The covenant with "many" refers to the unbelieving Jewish masses, rather than with any faithful remnant at that time. The "covenant" is not the covenant that will be made by the Lord as an everlasting covenant, Jer. 31.31, but is a covenant made by the future beast, "the prince that shall come" (thought by some to be Nero risen from the dead). This covenant will be the beast's contract with apostasy, supporting the anti-Christ in an effort to protect him and his territory from the king of the north, Dan. 11.40. Isaiah 28.15 is thought to refer to this, "We have made a covenant with death, and with hell are we at agreement; when the *overflowing scourge shall pass through.*" In other words, the protection ceases, and the northern power is victorious. The covenant is broken "in the midst of the week," leaving 3½ years for the course of the great tribulation. The Jewish ritual, "the sacrifice and the oblation," will cease, as in the days of Antiochus of old. Temple worship based on the O.T. pattern will cease. Anti-Christ will claim to be God, and will be worshipped, 2 Thess. 2.4, and Revelation 13 shows that he will still be in league with the Roman beast, even though the covenant has been broken.

The rest of verse 27 causes difficulties for translators. The "abominations" refer to idols; such an idol was referred to by the Lord Jesus in Matthew 24.15 as standing "in the holy place"—no doubt the image of the beast made by the anti-Christ, Rev. 13.14,15.

This state of affairs lasts for 3½ years, "until the consummation," the final consuming judgment of God that will rid the earth of such men and idols, "For the Lord God of hosts shall make a consumption (others translate this by *consummation*), even determined, in the midst of the land," Isa. 10.23. This consummation will be poured out on "the desolator," namely the Roman beast, Rev. 19.20. This will be the absolute end of the fourth kingdom; Daniel 12 follows with the day of resurrection of the martyrs.

Chapter 10
The Vision by the River Hiddekel

The Man Clothed in Linen, 10.1-9

1 Here is Daniel's last vision, taking place in the third year of Cyrus; chapters 10-12 form one connected vision. Chapter 10 is the preliminary to the details of the vision in chapters 11 and 12.

The background is found in Ezra 1. In the first year of Cyrus, many exiles had returned to Jerusalem, a decree by Cyrus allowing them to rebuild the temple, Ezra 1.3. In Daniel 9.25, the prophet had learned of "troublous times," without knowing the interpretation that 70 weeks equal 490 years, nor when these 70 weeks were to begin.

In the second year, they started rebuilding the temple, Ezra 3.8, but the people of the land "troubled them in building," 4.4, and they were frustrated "all the days of Cyrus," v.5. In fact, the temple was only finished about twenty years later, 6.15. Admittedly, the "troublous times" of Daniel 9.25 referred to the later rebuilding of the city, but Daniel must have been concerned about the present trouble in rebuilding the temple. Consequently the vision of chapters 10-12 was granted in his old age, partly to set his mind at rest.

This vision was "revealed"—namely, the source was from God. Men apparently still clung to the idolatrous name "Belteshazzar," but Scripture calls him properly "Daniel."

2 In grief, Daniel's exercise caused him to fast for three weeks (the context demands that these were actual weeks, not prophetic weeks of years as in 9.24). Once again, his prayer was heard **at the beginning** of these three weeks, v.12, reminding us of the previous chapter, verses 20,23, when Daniel had had a similar experience a few years before. By fasting, Daniel proved the Scripture that says, "man doth not live by bread alone, but by every word that proceedeth out of the mouth of the Lord doth man live," Deut. 8.3.

3   Daily necessities meant nothing to a man faced with such exercise before God. Of course, Daniel was refusing legitimate food, distinct from food that might be classified as excessive or too expensive, as he had refused from the king's court in his youth, Dan. 1.8. He was fasting so as the more to be able to hear the voice of God in his exercise, as prophets and teachers had fasted in Antioch so as to seek God's will for service, Acts 13.2. The anointing would be a sign of refreshment and joy, as in Ruth 3.3, where Noami gave instructions to Ruth; such anointing could not be used in a time of mourning, 2 Sam. 14.2. Of course, Daniel did not know how long this would have to last, but God commenced to answer from **the first day** that he started to chasten himself before God, Dan. 10.12. Direct intervention occurred after three weeks.

4   The passover (on the 14th day of the first month) and the week of the feast of unleavened bread occurred during these three weeks which ended on the 24th day of the first month (assuming this refers to the first month of the Jewish year). Daniel knew what it meant to "keep the feast, not with old leaven . . . but with the unleavened bread of sincerity and truth," 1 Cor. 5.8. This exercise of Daniel was accomplished by the river Hiddekel, namely the Tigris, one of the rivers that originally went out of Eden, Gen. 2.14, being about 50 miles from Babylon and the Euphrates. (The reader may seek to collect together all river scenes during the captivity, such as the captives sitting and weeping by the "rivers of Babylon," Psa. 137.1, and Ezekiel being found by the river Chebar, and seeing the heavens opened, Ezek. 1.1.)

5   He had been looking down as chastened, but then he looked up; he lifted up his eyes and saw the heavenly visitor. Until one is justified, one cannot lift up the eyes to heaven, as in the case of the publican, Luke 18.13. In the Lord's case, He lifted up His eyes from a scene of grief, John 11.41, as He also did in John 17.1 after having given His disciples His final teaching. For ourselves, we look upwards to the Lord Jesus, for by faith He is seen.

"Linen" denotes the righteous garments of a priest who discerns what is taking place. In Revelation 1.13, the Lord was "clothed with a garment down to the foot" as He discerned the state of the seven churches. In Leviticus 13.3 we read "the priest shall look" (occurring in several following verses), again denoting discerning power. The golden girdle, also seen in Revelation 1.13, appears in Isaiah 11.5, "righteousness shall be the girdle of his loins." The girdle is a sign of service, as in John 13.4; the gold speaks of the divine character of righteousness enabling Him to discern and to judge. (Some suggest that Uphaz is Ophir, as in Psalm 45.9, where we read of a queen "in gold of Ophir" at the right hand of the millennial throne of the Lord.)

6   The body of this "certain man" was "like the beryl" (though the exact nature of this precious stone is uncertain). The stone occurred in the fourth row of the high priests's breastplate, Exod. 28.20. In Ezekiel 1.16; 10.9, the wheels were of the colour of a beryl—the glory of God moving on inexorably in judgment. Moreover, the face of this "certain man" was "as the appearance of lightning," in its aspect of brightness rather than suddenness. Lightning is characteristic of several revelations, as on Sinai, Exod. 19.16, by the river Chebar, Ezek. 1.14, and from the throne in heaven, Rev. 4.5. Usually it denoted judicial divine intervention finding its mark. Here in our verse, it denotes the supreme dazzling glory of the man in linen, as in Matthew 17.2 where the kingdom glory of the Lord Jesus appeared "as the sun," and as in Acts 26.13 where the glory of the Lord as Head of the Church appeared to Paul "above the brightness of the sun."

His "eyes as lamps of fire" show piercing discernment, as on Patmos, Rev. 1.14. His arms and feet as "polished brass" did not, of course, indicate degredation as in the dream-image of Daniel 2, but showed the perfection of righteousness unaffected by world-conditions, as "his feet like unto fine brass, as if they burned in a furnace," Rev. 1.15; 2.18. His "voice . . . like the voice of a multitude" reminds us of the description "his voice as the sound of many waters," Rev. 1.15, and "his voice was like a noise of many waters," Ezek. 43.2, denoting the continuity of overwhelming purity and power. It is distinguished from a voice like a trumpet, which denotes a call to attention.

7   Only Daniel saw this vision; clearly it was a special vision for a special person under special circumstances. This was like the vision of Christ granted to Paul on the Damascus road; the others with him "stood speechless, hearing a voice, but seeing no man," Acts 9.7; (seeing a light, but not understanding the voice, 22.9). The divine presence was somehow recognized by those with Daniel—perhaps the noise of the voice. The fear was similar to the fear that fell on Moses and the people at Sinai, Exod. 20.18-21; Heb. 12.21. But the complete hiding of self from the divine presence was impossible, as witnessed elsewhere in Scripture, Gen. 3.10; Psa. 139.7-12; Luke 23.30; Rev. 6.16.

8   So Daniel was left alone, a position that God would sometimes have His people to be in, as was Jacob when he saw the ladder reaching up to heaven, Gen. 28.10-22; as was Moses in the desert when he saw the burning bush, Exod. 3.1-6, and many other examples.

The vision caused great physical and mental weakness in the old man. Thus the vision of the third heaven was tempered with the thorn in the flesh lest Paul should be exalted, 2 Cor. 12.7; Ezekiel fell upon his face at the sight of the glory of God, Ezek. 1.28, while John fell down at His feet as one dead when he saw the Lord on Patmos, Rev. 1.17.

9 The effect of *the sight* is described in verse 8, while the effect of *the sound* appears in verse 9 (both Paul and John were likewise moved by the sight and sound of the vision of Christ). Verse 8 led to a physical effect, but verse 9 to a mental effect as in a faint. Compare this with Peter and the others on the mount of transfiguration; they "were heavy with sleep," Luke 9.32.

Angelic Helpers, 10.10-21
10 The "man clothed in linen" is not mentioned again until Daniel 12.6. To be consistent, from our verse 10 onwards it is no longer the divine One of verses 5-9 that appears to Daniel, since he was "withstood" for twenty-one days, v.13, and had been helped by the arch-angel Michael. Possibly it is Gabriel who appears in verses 10-21 (who had already been manifested to Daniel in 8.16 and 9.21). This angelic being now ministered to Daniel in his need (angels had even ministered to the Lord after His temptation, Matt. 4.11), for angels are sent forth to minister to the heirs of salvation, Heb. 1.14. In Revelation 1.17 it was the Lord who laid His right hand upon John, but here it was the hand of this angelic speaker. He referred to Michael coming to help him, Dan. 10.13; later Daniel saw two others on the sides of the river, 12.5, after which the Man in linen spoke for the last time, v.7. (In 10.16, Daniel said, "O my lord," but in 12.8, he said, "O my *Lord*"—with a small *l* and a capital *L* respectively. The translators evidently concluded the one was an angel, but that the other was divine.)

11 The word "he" refers to the angel whose "hand" is mentioned in verse 10, distinct from the "arms" of the One clothed in linen in verse 6. Daniel is called "greatly beloved," as in 9.23 and 10.19. Here the word is a noun, but elsewhere it is an adjective: "*goodly* raiment," Gen. 27.15; "*precious* jewels," 2 Chron. 20.25; "*precious* as gold," Ezra 8. 27; "*pleasant* bread," Dan. 10.3; "*pleasant* things" in honour of a god by the anti-Christ, 11.38; "the *precious* things of Egypt" controlled by the king of the north, v. 43. So out of the nine times this word occurs, six appear in the Book of Daniel. It is properly translated "desirable," showing how God desired the faithfulness and service of Daniel.

The object of the revelation was that Daniel should "understand," though this does not imply that readers today should be able to understand every detail. The angel was "sent" for this purpose. Evangelists are "sent," Rom. 10.15, and so were the angels, such as "ministering spirits, sent forth," Heb. 1.14; "angels . . . that *do his commandments*," Psa. 103.20; Gabriel was *sent* to Zacharias and Mary, Luke 1.19,26. There are, of course, many examples of angelic appearances where the word "sent" is not used.

12 The angel said, "Fear not," an exhortation appearing in the Scriptures nearly 80 times, spoken by the Lord, by angels and by prophets. There is, of course, plenty of scope for the human mind and body to exhibit fear in the face of divine activity, and also on account of what the enemies of the gospel may do. But Daniel's prayer was heard immediately, even if there was no apparent answer outwardly. The reason why this prayer was heard was because there was a desire to understand on Daniel's part, because he had chastened himself, and on account of Daniel's words—all this was spiritual activity. Compare the N.T. conditions for prayer to be answered—we have provided a list in our comments on Daniel 9.18.

13 The reason for the three-week delay is now given. Usually, any delay can be attributed to the people's fault, such as in Isaiah 59.1,2 where the Lord will not hear because of the separation caused by iniquities and sins; James 1.6,7 where wavering and double-mindedness mean a lack of receiving from the Lord; and James 4.3,4 where the friendship of the world negates the value of prayer. But in our verse, "the prince of the kingdom of Persia" withstood Gabriel for three weeks. This was not Cyrus king of Persia who, as God's servant, had done all that he could for the rebuilding of the temple. It cannot stand for men generally, since one angel could deal with 185,000 Syrians in the days of Hezekiah, 2 Kings 19.35. Rather, such a "prince" would be Satanic power moving about amongst the nations. Such a power of evil had been working in Nebuchadnezzar and Belshazzar in Daniel chs. 3 and 5, The cruelty of the fourth beast, as prophesied in Daniel 7, was Satanic in origin, for the last beast ascends out of Satan's abode, the bottomless pit, Rev. 17.8. Similarly with the third beast, "the prince of Grecia," Dan. 10.20, refers to Satanic power. And in Matthew 4.9, Satan claimed authority over "all the kingdoms of the world." Nevertheless, God's will is done amongst the nations when He does not allow them to continue wholly in their own way.

When nations are infected by evil princes from Satan, God's angels ensure that His will is not overruled. (We may note the power of the dragon against the Jews in Revelation 12.15,17, yet help was at hand.) Thus Gabriel stated that Michael "one of the chief princes" or "the great prince," Dan. 12.1, came to help. Here was one exalted in power in the angelic hierarchy, his name meaning "Who is like God?" (the implication being, None, neither in heaven nor amongst Satan's forces). In Jude 9 he is called the "archangel," while he acts as head of the angelic forces directed against Satan himself, Rev. 12.7

14 The objective of the forthcoming prophecy was to let Daniel know what would happen to "thy people" (the Jews) in "the latter days." So chapter 11 leads up to this, finalized by the concluding details in chapter 12. Compare Daniel 9.24, where six features would be accomplished at the establishment of Messiah's kingdom at the end of the latter days.

15 At such words Daniel became a "dumb" prophet, his nervous system refused to function at such a revelation. How unlike the case of Zacharias who was struck dumb because of unbelief, Luke 1.20 (also when face to face with Gabriel), and that of Ezekiel who was dumb as a sign to an unbelieving people, Ezek. 3.26.

16 This "one like the similitude of the sons of men" cannot be identified with Christ, or Daniel would have noted that it was the Man clothed in linen. It was an angel in the form of a man (see Gen. 18.2; Heb. 13.2). Elsewhere the touching of lips was the work of the Lord, as Jeremiah 1.9 and Ezekiel 3.27, while in Isaiah 6.7 it was the work of a seraph; (so this lip-touching occurs in all four major prophets, with a different meaning in each case).

The result was that sorrows and pain came upon Daniel—even the beginning of the vision produced that effect. It shows the deep outcome that all this had on Daniel's frame. (The Hebrew word for "sorrows" occurs only five times: in 1 Samuel 4.19 literally as "pains" referring to childbirth, and in Isaiah 13.8; 21.3 metaphorically as "pangs.")

17 Daniel confessed that he was "the servant" of Gabriel, whom he called "my lord"; the particular Hebrew word used here, *adon*, is more often used of men, sometimes of God, and occasionally of an angel, Zech. 4.4. The word is often translated "master." We may ask, how could an old man in physical weakness talk to an angel? Evidently by the strengthening series of touches that he received, Dan. 10.10,16,18. In Biblical times, men were often allowed to talk with angels, such as Abraham, Gideon, Zacharias, Mary, for the word angel means "messenger."

18 Here is the third touch that Daniel received. In the Lord's miracles, one touch was always enough, except in the case of the blind man at Bethsaida, Mark 8.23-26, where two touches were used. After the first touch, the man saw "men as trees, walking," but after the second he "saw every man clearly." Namely, at conversion, there is still a lot to learn afterwards! In Daniel's case, the first touch caused him to stand trembling; the second touch opened his mouth to speak, while the third touch strengthened him so as to be able to receive the prophecy. The lesson to be learned is that conversion is followed by giving and receiving.

19 The great title "greatly beloved" or "greatly desired" now appears the third time in the Book of Daniel. The strength that Daniel received (in verses 18 and 19) arose from (i) the touch, and (ii) the words that Gabriel spoke. Only then was Daniel ready to receive the

vision of chapter 11. The same applies to ourselves; it is not *any* spiritual state that enables us to receive the message of the Lord. The things of God are spiritually discerned, 1 Cor. 2.14, and this demands a spiritual state, certainly not a carnal one. Paul was brought low in many ways, and then he could have the revelation of the third heaven, 2 Cor. 11.23 to 12.10.

20 Daniel's name does not occur until Daniel 12.4. The nations, and powerful men arising out of the nations, form the subject matter of the vision. Powerful angelic control amongst the nations was dictated by God; the angel's word was to ensure that God's will was done amongst the nations, so that Satanic princes of the nations could not resist God's will. The Satanic prince of Persia would have shown opposition to the decrees for the building of the temple and city; in both cases there was trouble, Ezra 4.4; Neh. 4.1. The work would have succumbed to Satan's ravages had there not been this angelic help.

The angel had come forth to reveal prophetic truth to Daniel, yet he had exercised power against the prince of Persia, and also had anticipated that the prince of Greece would later cause trouble amongst the Jews, as actually happened in chapter 11. These princes would be amongst those whom Paul called "principalities, powers, rulers of the darkness of the world, spiritual wickedness in high places," Eph. 6.12. (**Note:** the order Persia — Greece is always maintained in chapters 2,7,8,11, being the historical order in which the events took place after Daniel's life was over.)

21 "I will show thee that which is noted in the scripture of truth" denotes the source of the revelation of chapter 11. It cannot refer to the O.T. (although this is indeed composed of the Scriptures of truth), since the details in chapter 11 were not in the O.T. as existing in Daniel's day. It must refer to God's book of divine foreknowledge. Thus in this (or another) book were written all the members of the physical body of the psalmist David even *before* his birth, Psa. 139.16; David's tears of sufferings were in God's bottle, namely "in thy book," 56.8. God's book also contained the remembrance of the faithful ones, who feared the Lord and spoke often one to another, Mal. 3.16.

The only one to help Gabriel in his work was "Michael your prince," namely an angel from heaven as distinct from a power from Satan. He had a special responsibility for the Jewish nation, as Daniel 12.1 shows, for he is "the great prince which standeth for the children of thy people." Whatever men and Satan may do on earth, there is comfort in the fact that God has His means for the care and ultimate blessing of His people.

Chapter 11
The Activity of the King of the North

The details occurring in this vision commence a few years earlier in the first year of Darius (the vision was given in the third year of the following king Cyrus). Verses 1 and 2 provide some brief references to the second kingdom, that of Persia. In verses 3 to 32, we have a detailed account of relationships between the king of the north (Syria and the north-east) and the king of the south (Egypt and the south-west), with the land to Judaea and Jerusalem wedged in between. Most expositors see these verses as prophetic history of the third kingdom leading up to Antiochus Epiphanes king of Syria. Other expositors feel that all these details refer to events after the rapture. But it must be admitted that historians agree that verses 3 to 32 correspond exactly to historical events that took place over the four centuries between Daniel and Antiochus, so that theologians who reject the miraculous in prophecy insist that the Book of Daniel was written *after* all these events were over!

We believe that prophecy was often given **locally in time** so as to refer to events **far-distant in time**. The history of these past four centuries can indeed be traced in detail in these verses, as a **signpost** to future events (perhaps not in minute detail, but in principle) during the last 70th week of prophecy.

Thus in verses 3 to 32 we see how the land was (and will be) used by political and military rivals. In B.C. 538 we have Darius, the first king of the second empire. In B.C. 336 we have Alexander the Great, the first king of the third empire of Greece. In B.C. 176 Antiochus Epiphanes became king of Syria, while in the period B.C. 170-165 we have the sufferings of the Jews under Antiochus; his deeds are described in verses 21 to 32. The present author is not a historian, so the very brief details on verses 3 to 32 have been extracted from the more extensive writings of others.

Verses 33 to 35 form "bridging" verses, a survey of Jewish experience up to the end times. Verses 36 to 45 describe an evil personage of future days, and what he will endure at the hands of the king of the north. We interpret this evil personage as being an antitype of the little horn of Daniel 8.9, as explained in chapter 8.

Chapter 12 deals with the great tribulation, with resurrection at the end, and with certain periods of time during this last 70th week of prophecy.

Introduction, 11.1,2

1   Gabriel asserted that his protective power defended Darius the first king of the Medo-Persian empire right from his first year. "The prince of Persia" had been a Satanic force in opposition to the purpose of God being done, so Darius and then Cyrus needed protection.

2   The three kings who followed Cyrus were Ahasuerus, Ezra 4.6; Artaxerxes, 4.7-23; Darius II, 4.24. The next king, Ahasuerus (Xerxes), Esther 1.1, used an army of over two million men to attack Greece, but was himself defeated, though after that the kingdom of Persia remained for longer than a century, until the third kingdom of Greece became dominant in the world.

Warfare and Intrigue up to Antiochus Epiphanes, 11.3-32

In verse 3, we have Alexander the Great (the "notable horn" in 8.5), who died at an early age, v.4. Four generals took over, none of whom was of Alexander's posterity. Prophecy is now focussed on Egypt and Syria with Judaea located in between, v.5. Ptolemy I was the Greek general who was allocated Egypt as his kingdom. One of his officers, Seleucus I, succeeded him with an extended kingdom. Ptolemy II of Egypt made peace with Antiochus II of Syria, v.6, by means of the marriage of Ptolemy's daughter Berenice to Antiochus II after his divorce. Ptolemy II died, and his former wife Laodice had Antiochus and Berenice put to death—here was interfamily and international intrigue. Berenice's brother Ptolemy III therefore invaded Syria, v.7, conquered the country and put Laodice to death. Ptolemy III returned to Egypt with vast treasures, v.8, including "their gods" to denote complete subjugation of the defeated country.

On his return to Egypt, he did not take advantage of his conquest over Syria, v.8, so Antiochus III of Syria became great, and inflicted losses on Ptolemy IV of Egypt, v.10. In retaliation, Syria was again defeated, v.11. This useless life of Ptolemy IV led to the persecution of the Jews in Egypt, because he was not allowed to enter within the vail in the temple in Jerusalem, v.12. Antiochus III gathered a large army against Egypt, because the new boy king Ptolemy V was only four years old, v.13. Antiochus III gained victories, establishing headquarters in Judaea, the glorious land, vs. 14-16. He gave his daughter Cleopatra to young Ptolemy V so as to gain Egypt by subtlety, v. 17, but she refused to act against Egypt, maintaining loyalty to her husband. Antiochus then turned his attention to the Mediterranean isles and coasts, v.18, but was defeated by the Romans in B.C. 190. He returned humiliated to his own land, and was killed by the Persians, v.19. His son raised taxes in Syria for the Romans, and his taxgatherer even tried to plunder the temple in Jerusalem, v.20, but this man then poisoned the king.

His son Antiochus IV Epiphanes (the illustrious one), v.21, became king of Syria (up to verse 32) being the same as the "little horn" of 8.9. He was a "vile person" or "contemptible person," being greedy, cunning, of violent passions and doing deeds of great public shame. He smashed Egypt, v.22, which was seeking to reconquer lost territory. He made a subtle "covenant" with Ptolemy VI of Egypt (some suggest that it was with the high priest Onias in Jerusalem). Behind this friendship, he took the whole of Egypt except Alexandria, v.23. The spoil was distributed to his followers and people, v.24. We then have a battle in Egypt between Antiochus and Ptolemy VI, v.25, but Ptolemy was overthrown by his own subjects, v.26, so Antiochus and Ptolemy planned reconquest, v.27. Antiochus returned through Palestine, v.28, and acted against the holy land and its people. He killed tens of thousands in Jerusalem, stole treasures from within the temple vail, and sacrificed a swine on the altar.

At a time permitted by God, Antiochus invaded Egypt again, v.29, but the Egyptians obtained help from the Romans, v.30. Antiochus returned to Syria humiliated, taking revenge on Jerusalem. He killed thousands, caused the temple worship to cease, v.31, set fire to the city, and insisted on worship only to the Greek god Jupiter, himself being regarded as a god (reminding us of 2 Thessalonians 2.4). He erected an altar for a heathen god, and faithful Jews were tortured if they did not observe it. The altar and its idol formed "the abomination that maketh desolate." In Matthew 24.15, the Lord Jesus did not refer to this **historical** event, but to a worse **future** event—namely, the antitype of the deed of Antiochus, and to Daniel 12.11 which is certainly future. Antiochus gained the apostate Jews, v.32, but the faithful remnant stood firm (described in 1 and 2 Maccabees in the Apocrypha).

The Bridging Verses, 11.33-35

If the previous verses are taken to refer to the historical events just described, then we understand verses 33 to 35 to be general verses relating to events from Antiochus up to the time of the great tribulation after the rapture. But if the previous verses are taken to refer solely to the future, then verses 33 to 35 also refer to that time.

In verse 33, the faithful ones maintain spiritual teaching, so as to preserve the testimony (as those in Revelation 11.3,4, and as has happened many times through the Christian era). Yet they fall "by the sword, and by flame, by captivity"; thus they were burnt alive in caves, 2 Macc. 6.11; Heb. 11.35-37, awaiting the resurrection of Daniel 12.2.

The restoration of temple service is not noticed; in any case, it was obliterated in A.D. 70. The verses blend with the end times, as the words "many days" and "even to the time of the end" demonstrate.

Verses 34 and 35 trace the persecution of the Jews throughout history. Strange things take place. Other men will cleave to them falsely, and will be found wanting; such will be rooted out leaving the faithful ones "white." Such false testimony makes these men to be of the "synagogue of Satan"—those who say they are Jews and are not, Rev. 3.9; Matt. 7.22,23; Acts 20.29; Gal. 2.4.

The Anti-Christ and the King of the North, 11.36-45

These closing verses show the relationship between the anti-Christ and the king of the north in the final years after the rapture. Those who see nothing really prophetic in such a paragraph state that Antiochus is still being described, but the "king" in verse 36 must be distinct from the "king of the north" in verse 40, since warfare between them is outlined. Some have said that this "king" in verse 36 denotes the pope and Rome, but these events take place in Palestine (as shown by "the glorious land," v.41), so such an identification is not possible. In the Book of Revelation, Mystery Babylon, 17.5, denotes the fully matured Romish system, not the anti-Christ who is described as "the false prophet." Rather, the description in Daniel 11.36-39 answers to the anti-Christ seeking self-deification.

36   "The king shall do according to his will," or "the wilful king" is a
      man completely defiant to the will of God. Satan, as Lucifer, had this character in Isaiah 14.13,14, saying five times, "*I will* ascend . . . *I will* exalt . . . *I will* sit . . . *I will* ascend . . . *I will* be like the most High." Such an attitude is not unknown in the world today; the spirit of anti-Christ is already in the world, 1 John 4.3, and "the mystery of iniquity doth already work," 2 Thess. 2.7.

"He shall exalt himself . . . above every god." This has been characteristic of the Roman emperors, of Herod, Acts 12.22,23, and of the doctrine of some of the Roman popes. No doubt this future anti-Christ will use the wonders of modern science as well as Satanic power to achieve his exaltation, for "he doeth great wonders . . . and deceiveth them . . . by means of those miracles which he had power to do," Rev. 13.13,14. Paul warned that the man of sin "exalteth himself above all that is called God," 2 Thess. 2.4.

He "shall speak marvellous things against the God of gods." This has been the practice of false theology and of heresies over the centuries. In his doctrine, he will show "himself that he is God," 2 Thess. 2.4, forming part of a rebellious apostate doctrine that will be imposed upon the Jews. Such a false prophet will endeavour, if possible, to deceive even the very elect, Matt. 24.24. In this activity and doctrine, he "shall prosper till the indignation be accomplished," that is, the great tribulation, being the wrath of God upon men, and the wrath of evil men upon the faithful ones. See Daniel 8.19; 12.1; Matt. 24.21.

37   He will not "regard the God of his fathers." This is a Jewish expression; the anti-Christ will entirely reject the historically revealed God of Abraham, Isaac and Jacob, and hence all the revealed Word concerning the divine Person. This is the man of sin, "coming . . . after the working of Satan," 2 Thess. 2.9. Such a man would be of his father the devil, far from having God as Father, John 8.42.

"Nor the desire of women." Expositors make various suggestions about this phrase, since its meaning is not stated. The suggestions include the papal requirement of celibacy in its priesthood. Rather, the desire of Jewish women would be to give birth to the Messiah, but this concept will be rejected entirely by the anti-Christ. Of course, this desire of such women would demonstrate complete ignorance, since the Messiah had been born long ago, Luke 2.7, and His next advent will be in judgment and glory.

"Nor regard any god," since he will claim to be God. He will exalt himself above all, to emulate the pre-eminent position of Christ on high.

38   Rather, he will "honour the god of forces (or fortresses)," evidently referring to Satan as the god of this world, as the prince of the power of the air, as cast out into the earth with his angels, Rev. 12.9. The anti-Christ will be motivated and activated by Satan, as was Judas, John 13.2. The faithful fathers of old kept far from Satan in their spiritual devotions, since they worshipped the true God who revealed Himself to them. During the temptation in the wilderness, the Lord Jesus could not and would not worship Satan, but the anti-Christ will worship the dragon in that day. This worship will use material things as gold and silver, copying the symbolism of the tabernacle and temple of old, and also copying the spiritual realities of the service of believers today, 1 Cor. 3.12. As sitting in the temple, 2 Thess. 2.4, he will prepare this for Satan as a copy of God's typology of old, making it like the house of Dagon, and like Jeroboam's "house of high places" to attract the people, 1 Kings 12.31. By these materialistic devices, he will seek to deceive the people, as did Simon of Samaria, Acts 8.9.

39   Some suggest that the reference to "strong holds" denotes the anti-Christ's glorying in war. Rather, it appears to refer to man-

made religious sanctuaries and structures, as places for the worship of Satan, like "the synagogue of Satan," Rev. 2.9; 3.9. In one there will be set up an image of the emperor of the fourth kingdom, 13.14.

He will "increase with glory" this strange god. This is a copy of the Christian's true attitude to Christ: "He must increase," John 3.30. By this means he will attempt to recreate Satan's original glory and beauty described in Ezekiel 28.1-19.

The last part of verse 39 appears to denote confederates of anti-Christ; they will benefit under the distribution of power granted by the anti-Christ. In apostate times, there are always men willing to adhere to a false leader, so as to participate in the corruption of power devolved to favourites of the leader. Thus in 1 Kings 1.5, there were 50 men ready to run before Adonijah when he usurped power, including the general Joab and the high priest Abiathar. See Acts 5.36,37; 21.38.

40   We now come to the activity of the king of the north (Syria) and the king of the south (Egypt). The antagonism of the past will be renewed in the future. There is power in the hands of the king of the north as he invades many countries. It appears that the "covenant" in Daniel 9.27 between Israel and Rome will be for the protection of the Israeli state from the invasions of the kings of the north and the south. But when this covenant is disannulled, then the king of the north shall "overflow and pass over."

41   In this overflowing process, the king of the north will enter "the glorious land," the land that was once God's kingdom in the days of David and Solomon. But as he spreads out, he will avoid Edom (Esau), and Moab and Ammon (Lot), nations that were derived as off-shoots of the early family in Genesis. All through the O.T., they were enemies of the Jews, so the king of the north treats them favourably. However, the major prophets trace their judgment, and they still await this future judgment of God: "the sword of the Lord," Isa. 34.6; "I will bring a fear upon thee," Jer. 49.5; "I will stretch out my hand upon thee," Ezek. 25.7.

42,43   All the neighbouring countries will suffer at his hand—he emulates the expansionism of the fourth beast. All the treasures and wealth of Egypt (that Moses refused, Heb. 11.26) will be taken as booty—perhaps including all engineering expertise and products. In the past, Satan offered the Lord Jesus all the valuable things of the kingdoms of the world, but was rebuked; in the future, this king of the north will take all that is within his grasp.

44   At this time, the beast will be locked in warfare with the hoards from beyond the river Euphrates—at the battle of Armageddon, Rev. 16.12. Hearing this news, the king of the north will still be intent upon preserving his own territory and that gained by his own invasions.

45 He will even judge it best to make mount Zion his headquarters—"the glorious holy mountain." At that stage the Lord
will come in judgment and glory. The Stone will break the iron and clay
of the fourth kingdom, Dan. 2.45. All nations will be gathered against
Jerusalem, Zech. 14.2. The Lord will "fight against those nations," and
His feet shall stand on the mount of Olives, vs. 3,4. The Lord "will smite
all the people that have fought against Jerusalem," v.12, and all the
wealth will be gathered into that city, v.14.

Those who make war against the Lamb, Rev. 17.14, will be overcome
by the Lamb. The king of the north "shall come to his end, and none shall
help him"; the beast and the anti-Christ (as the false prophet) will be
slain, Rev. 19.20; Dan. 7.11; 8.25. Such judgment upon the national
leaders and their armies will be a necessary prelude for Messiah's
kingdom of peace to be established, for the kingdom will be brought in
by these processes of divine judgment. Only those who revere and study
God's Word see that this will be so; mere religionists speak of nothing
but divine love.

Chapter 12
The Great Tribulation

The Great Tribulation, 12.1-4

This chapter deals with the great tribulation and events that take place afterwards, particularly that of resurrection. It is provided to give hope to those in the future who have to pass through these years of terror and persecution.

1   The details of the great tribulation have been provided in verses 36-45 of the previous chapter, but now there is no reference to the kings of the north and south. Here this period is called "a time of trouble," and its uniqueness is stressed by the description "such as never was since there was a nation even to that same time." In Matthew 24.21, the Lord called the period "great tribulation," again stressing the uniqueness of the event, "such as was not since the beginning of the world to this time, no, nor ever shall be." Verses 16-25 describe this time, to be marked by false Christs and false prophets with "great signs and wonders." In verse 29 it is called "the tribulation of those days," followed immediately afterwards by a catastrophe of signs in heaven preceding the coming of the Son of man in glory. In Mark 13.19, this period is called "affliction," with its uniqueness described. In Revelation 7.14, it is called "great tribulation," and many martyrs are seen standing before the throne. In Jeremiah 30.7, occurring before paragraphs of restorative blessings, this period is called "the time of Jacob's trouble," its uniqueness being defined by the words, "that day is great, so that none is like it." In Revelation 3.10, it is called "the hour of temptation."

During this time of trouble, God provides an archangel to stand for "thy people" the Jews. The archangel's power to do this has been recorded in Daniel 10.13, where he was able to stand against the Satanic prince of Persia. (Others too will stand for the persecuted Jews, such as the "sheep" in the Lord's parable in Matthew 25.33-40, "Inasmuch as ye have done it unto one of the least of these my brethren, ye have done it unto me"; see Rev. 12.16. In Jude 9, Michael is the only named archangel in Scripture, and since he was in attendance over the body of Moses, it may be that he will be in attendance at the resurrection of believers in the church, 1 Thess. 4.16. In Daniel 10.13, he was "one of the chief princes" engaged in providing powerful help against the Satanic prince of Persia. In Revelation 12.7-9, it is through Michael that Satan is cast down to earth, admittedly to engage in the terrors of the great tribulation for 3½ years, but Michael will also be there to preserve the faithful Jews. This preservation will be two-fold: (i) to preserve some alive to enter into the kingdom of Christ, and (ii) those who are martyred until the resurrection at the end of that period. All are "written in the book," no doubt one of those mentioned in Daniel 7.10 and Revelation 20.12 (though these are used on different occasions).

2 This verse contains a clear O.T. statement on the resurrection: "many of them that sleep in the dust of the earth shall awake." Some suggest that this refers to the national restoration of Israel, such as the valley of dry bones yielding life again, Ezek. 37.1-14: "I will open your graves, and cause you to come up out of your graves," v.12. This is perfectly true, and is a very suitable metaphor. But our verse also states "and some to shame and everlasting contempt." This does not appear to have national non-restoration in view, since eternal consequences are mentioned. Rather, we believe that the reference is to the first resurrection that takes place at the end of the great tribulation, Rev. 20.4-6; the rest of the dead will not live until the "second resurrection" in readiness for the final judgment at the great white throne. The distinction between these two types of resurrection was also made by the Lord Jesus, "all that are in the graves shall hear his voice, and shall come forth: they that have done good, unto the resurrection of life; and they that have done evil, unto the resurrection of damnation," John 5.28,29.

3 Spiritual leaders at that time receive special notice. The "wise" (or, teachers, marg.) and those that "turn many to righteousness" will, after their prior martyrdom, possess the resurrection state described here. Natural wisdom is discounted throughout Scripture, Matt. 11.25; 1 Cor. 1.19; 2.5. Only spiritual wisdom is of value—"the wisdom of God" and "the word of wisdom" given by the Spirit, 1 Cor. 2.7; 12.8. In this future day, the wisdom of teachers will involve the understanding and application of the prophetic Scriptures; armed with this they will be able to guide others to righteousness. It will form part of the "gospel of the kingdom" to be preached in all the world before the end comes, Matt. 24.14. For example, the two witnesses in Revelation 11.3-12 can be so described; they will be martyred, and their special resurrection and ascent to heaven will be watched by their enemies, v.12.

Resurrection is characterized by glory and eternity—"as the stars for ever and ever." The picture used is that of purity and brightness, though never eclipsing the "Sun of righteousness," Mal. 4.2, the One whose "face did shine as the sun," Matt. 17.2. Yet the blessed Lord shares His glory, John 17.22, so in that day "shall the righteous shine forth as the sun in the kingdom of their Father," Matt. 13.43.

4   Daniel had to "seal the book" up to the "time of the end." On the other hand, John did not have to seal the Book of Revelation "for the time is at hand," Rev. 22.10. Daniel had to arrange for the contents of his Book to be preserved; he had no idea when the end would come. John had to publicize his Book, since the Lord was coming quickly. Yet Daniel's Book was not to be hidden; it would be investigated from end to end by "many." To "run to and fro" means "to investigate," as in Zechariah 4.10, where "the eyes of the Lord . . . run to and fro through the whole earth." On account of this investigation of prophecy, "knowledge shall be increased"—knowledge obtained by searching the prophetic Scriptures. By this means, our knowledge of Christ increases, as does our knowledge of Paul's teaching and of the prophetic word, John 5.29; Acts 17.11; 2 Pet. 1.19,20.

Daniel's Last Looking and Hearing, 12.5-13

5   Two more angels appeared, one on each side of the river Hiddekel, clearly in addition to the angelic speaker in the previous two chapters. They were under the control of the Man clothed in linen who had been above the waters since 10.5. The river is no barrier to divine authority, though rivers are often barriers to men in their expansionism and warfare, Rev. 16.12.

6   One angel addressed the Man clothed in linen who occupied the heavenly position "above" (rather than "upon") the river. The Lord was ever elevated, and will remain so until His feet touch the mount of Olives in the future day, Zech. 14.4. The question asked by the angel was, "How long?", the same question that must have been in Daniel's mind. In Daniel 9.2, he knew the duration of the captivity was to be 70 years; in 9.24 he knew that the prophetic message spanned 70 weeks, though, being ignorant of the year in which Messiah would die, he did not know how these weeks could be translated into years. Here, he finally wanted to know the duration of the great tribulation, in just the same way as the martyrs asked, "How long?" Rev. 6.10.

7   To answer this question, the glorious One swore by Him that lives for ever; this was an attestation, by act and word, of the truth of the answer. In Genesis 14.22, Abram lifted up *his hand* to the Lord; in Revelation 10.5,6, and angel lifted up *his hand* and swore "by him that liveth for ever and ever." But here in our verse, the glorious One

lifted up *both hands*, to swear "by him that liveth for ever and ever." In other words, One divine swears by One divine. This reminds us of Hebrews 6.13,14, "when God made promise to Abraham, because he could swear by no greater, he sware *by himself*, saying, Surely blessing I will bless thee," the idiom being such that the oath is contained in the words "Surely I."

What was being so solemnly attested was the *finite* duration of the great tribulation; it would last only for "a time, times, and half a time," namely 3½ years, or half the duration of the 70th week. This same period is called 1,260 days (for testimony), Rev. 11.3, and also the time in which the woman (the Jews) has to flee into the wilderness, 12.6; this same period is called "a time, and times, and half a time" in 12.14, while the beast had power for 42 months, 13.5; 11.2.

The end of this period will also be the time "when he shall have accomplished to scatter the power of the holy people." It is God who has scattered, and who allows to be scattered, this "*holy* people." At the beginning, they were called "an *holy* nation," Exod. 19.6; "ye shall be *holy* unto me: for I . . . have severed you from other people, that ye should be mine," Lev. 20.26; "thou art an *holy* people unto the Lord," Deut. 7.6. Yet they had been scattered during the Babylonian captivity (the opposite thought to "severed from"), losing their power or authority in Jerusalem; they were scattered in due time after the Lord's crucifixion, with the branches having been broken off the olive tree because of unbelief, Rom. 11.20. And in the second half of the last week (the last 3½ years) Satan too seeks to persecute and to scatter, Rev. 12.13 17.

This continues to take place until "all *these things* shall be finished," namely when all the references in chapters 7,8,9,11,12 to the political, religious, military and Satanic activity against God's people are finished. This will occur when "the times of the Gentiles be fulfilled," Luke 21.24. Certainly the days will be shortened, else none would escape, Matt. 24.22, shortened according to the prearranged program of God. The martyrs who cry "How long?", Rev. 6.10,11, must await their resurrection, until the season "should be fulfilled" in which the rest of the martyrs suffer death. Here is comfort for those who suffer—the time of their tribulation is limited, and the scattering will be over when "the angels . . . shall gather together his elect from the four winds, from one end of heaven to the other," Matt. 24.31. Thus blessing is at hand when these things are at the doors, v.33; namely, when the great tribulation is in progress, the end is near.

8 Daniel only had partial understanding. With the N.T. in our hands, we have further light. There will be even further understanding when God's people in these future days can relate actual events with these prophetical words of warning and of comfort. So

Daniel asked for the circumstances of "the end," namely, the end of the dominion of man, and the beginning of the authority of Christ in His kingdom.

9   As far as Daniel was concerned, "the words are closed and seal-ed," namely the time of fulfilment would not be in Daniel's day, but only at the "time of the end." Consequently, unfulfilled prophecy had to be closed and sealed—not to be hidden from readers, but to re-main preserved and ready to be fulfilled when the time arrives. It is preserved for Christians today, so that they can appreciate this prophecy in the light of additional N.T. revelation. It is preserved for God's people after the rapture, so that they can see light at the end of a short but bitter tunnel, seeing the predicted events unfolding before their eyes, yet know-ing that all enmity against them will shortly be dissipated under the judgments of God. At the same time, another sealed book appears in heaven, Rev. 5.1, to be unsealed by the Lamb during this last 70th week.

10   Being purified and made white is the blessed prerogative of believers over the centuries, whenever forgiveness is available to faith. But this verse refers to the future, when these blessings are linked with being "tried" by the events brought about by men and Satan. In this 70th week, spiritual testimony after the rapture will spread, for example, by the two witnesses in Revelation 11.3, when the "gospel of the kingdom shall be preached in all the world for a witness unto all nations," Matt. 24.14. Those who take heed will be purged and made white, as one of the 24 elders said to John, "These are they which came out of great tribulation, and have washed their robes, and made them white in the blood of the Lamb," Rev. 7.14.

A faith such as this will lead to many being "tried" during this "time of trouble," namely during "the tribulation the great" as the Greek text of Revelation 7.14 puts it. But the majority of men will present a contrast; the wicked ones (in the plural) will continue in their wickedness, as the Lord said to John in His very last words in recorded Scripture, "He that is unjust, let him be unjust still: and he which is filthy, let him be filthy still," Rev. 22.11. In other words, truth is not forced into the hearts of unwilling men, neither today nor in that future day. It will be impossible for the wicked to understand, since sin clouds the mind. Only "the wise" will understand, but the Lord adds that the righteous and the holy ones remain in righteousness and holiness. In other words, at that time there will be a complete moral and spiritual separation on earth, like the wheat from the tares, Matt. 13.24-30, even though both grow together; when the Lord comes in glory, He will enforce their separation finally and eternally.

11   This act of anti-Christ, in setting up his idolatrous image in the temple, and refusing to allow the daily sacrifice, is a time-pointer in the last 70th week; see Matt. 24.15. There remain 1,290 days. (Some say that there were 1,290 days between Antiochus' desecration of the temple up to the restoration of its service, and that the 1,335 days in verse 12 denote the period from this desecration of the temple up to the death of Antiochus, but this is merely the speculation of unbelief in unfulfilled prophecy.) Rather, Daniel chapter 12 deals with the future; the last half week is of 1,260 days duration (or 42 months, or 3½ years). Another 30 days have been added to this, up to the termination of an unspecified event.

12 Blessing comes after 1,335 days, namely another 45 days have been added. Again, Scripture does not define what these days refer to. Some expositors make no suggestions, others present ideas. These days may be needed for the overthrow of all the nations when the Lord comes in glory, for the destruction of the king of the north, for the judgment of the living nations, Matt. 25.31-46, and for the introduction of millennial administration. These 30 and 45 days are not mentioned in Matthew 24, though they would occur in verses 29 to 31. The intervention of the Lamb at the battle of Armageddon in Revelation 17.14, and the final overthrow of the beasts in chapter 19, are events separated by those in chapter 18, and this may require the extra 75 days. Time is also needed to cleanse the earth of the effects of judgment, Rev. 14.18-20; 19.21, when "all the fowls are filled with their flesh," 19.17,21.

13 This last verse is personal to Daniel at the end of his life. "Go thou thy way" is the way of all men. Joshua said, "I am going the way of all the earth," Josh. 23.14; David said, "I go the way of all the earth," 1 Kings 2.2. So Daniel's body rests in the grave, until his resurrection day, when he shall "stand in thy lot at the end of the days." Namely, he will be amongst the "many" of Daniel 12.2 (though distinguish between the resurrection of men of faith at the rapture, and of those raised at "the first resurrection" at the end of the 70th week). The word "lot" (from the casting of a lot) was a designation given to the portions of land distributed by Joshua, Judg. 1.3. So, too, in Daniel's case; his "lot" denotes his resurrection position in blessing on account of his faithfulness, no doubt referring to the thrones in Revelation 20.4, occupied by those who had not worshipped the beast.

So the Book of Daniel closes full of hope, both for those who pass on at all times through the centuries, and for those who are martyred at the end times. For the "lot" is but a prelude to the eternal kingdom, unaffected by the enemies of the cross of Christ. God's purpose in ultimate deliverance remains certain, as Job 42.2. R.V. puts it, "I know that thou canst do all things, and that no purpose of thine can be restrained."

Verses in Daniel still to be fulfilled

2. 33-35   The vision of the last kingdom and the kingdom of the Stone.

2. 41-45   The interpretation of this part of the vision

4. 3,34   The everlasting nature of God's kingdom (Nebuchadnezzar)

6. 26   The everlasting nature of God's kingdom (Darius)

7. 8-14,18, 20-27   The future kingdom of the fourth beast, followed by the eternal kingdom of the Son of man

8. 9-12   Dream-type of the anti-Christ yet to come

8. 23-25   Interpretation referring to the future of the king of the north

9. 24, 26end, 27   The last 70th week and the subsequent blessings

11. 5-35   Past history used as a signpost to future events — wars between north and south across Jewish territory

11. 36-45   Warfare between the anti-Christ and the king of the north

12. 1-4   The great tribulation and subsequent resurrection

12. 7-13   Certainty that the great tribulation will come to its end